PARTICIPATORY COMMUNITY WORK

About the Author

Dr. Zubair Meenai is presently a Professor at the Department of Social Work and Dean, Students' Welfare, Jamia Millia Islamia, New Delhi (a Central University). He has extensive experience of working on participatory projects and has served as Project Implementation Expert in the World Bank and IFAD supported Rural Women's Development and Empowerment Project (Swa-Shakti). Prior to this he has worked as Fellow at the LBS National Academy of Administration, Mussoorie. He has served as social sector analyst to various appraisal missions of the District Primary Education Programme. Dr Meenai is also the Director of a UNICEF supported community based 'Advocacy and Networking for Health among Under-Served' Project in western Uttar Pradesh as well as of the Women's Development Centre in the Jamia Millia Islamia. He serves as Programme Advisor to the State Resource Centre for Literacy for Delhi. He is also responsible for the Child Rights Programme in the university. Dr. Meenai has been a consultant to many NGOs in the field of participatory methodologies, micro-credit, self help groups and women's empowerment. His other publications include 'Empowering Rural Women: An Approach to Empowering Women through Credit-Based Self Help Groups' (Aakar Books). He can be contacted at zmeenai@gmail.com.

PARTICIPATORY COMMUNITY WORK

Zubair Meenai

CONCEPT PUBLISHING COMPANY, NEW DELHI-110059

Cataloging in Publication Data—DK
Courtesy: D.K. Agencies (P) Ltd. <docinfo@dkagencies.com>

Meenai, Zubair, 1964-
Participatory community work / Zubair Meenai.
p. cm.
In Indian context.
Includes bibliographical references (p.)
Includes index.
ISBN 13: 9788180694097
ISBN 10: 8180694097

1. Social service—India—Citizen participation. 2. Community development—India. I. Title.

DDC 362.095 4 22

ISBN -13: 978-81-8069-409-7
ISBN -10: 81-8069-409-7

First Published 2008

Published and Printed by
Ashok Kumar Mittal
Concept Publishing Company
A/15-16, Commercial Block, Mohan Garden
New Delhi (INDIA)

Phones : 25351460, 25351794
Fax : 091-11-25357103
Email : publishing@conceptpub.com

'Would you tell me please, which way I ought to go from here?'

'That depends a good deal on where you want to get to', said the cat.

'I don't much care where', said Alice.

'Then it doesn't matter which way you go', said the cat.

—Alice in Wonderland, Lewis Carroll

Preface

Over the past two decades or so, a number of innovations in techniques and areas of intervention have been made in the field of social development. Prominent among them are the participatory approaches and the rights based approach. These approaches and interventions have made creditable impact on the lives of the poor. Consequently, these have found favour with a number of governmental and non-governmental actors. It is however seen that professional social work is following an almost parallel trajectory and has not been able to integrate such approaches in its ambit. Thus, there is a need for the two to converge. There also exists a need to critically examine the concept of community work in the Indian context and attempt to integrate participatory and rights-based concerns with social work practice and community work. This book attempts the same by delineating participatory techniques and the rights based approach and integrate them with community work as a method of social work.

During the course of writing of this book, I have benefited from various existing writings and formulations and have freely borrowed from them to present my argument in a particular way. Throughout this venture, my understanding of the framework has been strengthened by constant interactions with my colleagues and peers. I owe thanks to Razdan Sarim Rahman for his critical and practical inputs with the tools and also for acting as a sounding board. I would also like to thank the students of the Department of Social Work, Jamia Millia Islamia, who have successfully tried out these tools in the rural Camp-2006. Thanks are also due to my friend and colleague, Dr Archana Dassi, for providing me with encouragement. Most importantly, I am indebted to my wife, Dr Sheema Aleem for her constant encouragement and support. Her spirited cooperation and pleasant companionship provided me with sustained energy to complete this task. Finally, I would like to acknowledge Mr Ashok Kumar Mittal of Concept Publishing Company for bringing out this production without any reservations.

Zubair Meenai

Contents

Preface vii

List of Box, Figures and Tables xi

1. Contemporary Social Work and Community Work 1
2. Participation and the Participatory Approach 39
3. Attitudes and Skills in Participatory Community Work 68
4. Participatory Tools and Methods 98
5. Participatory Monitoring and Evaluation 135

Annexes

Annex-I 164
Annex-II 168
Annex-III 175
Annex-IV 178
Annex-V 189
Annex-VI 196

References 213

Index 222

List of Box, Figures and Tables

Box

1 Ideal Community 15

Figures

1 Three Perspectives of Participation 48
2 Project Cycle 56
3 Rights Based Approach to Development 69
4 Linking PRA to LFA 92
5 Resource Map 101
6 Social Map 103
7 Transect Walk 106
8 Well-Being Analysis 108
9 Seasonal Calendar 110
10 Daily Activity Clock (Men) 112
11 Daily Activity Clock (Women) 113
12 Mobility Map 114
13 Venn Diagram 117
14 Trend Lines 118
15 Pair-Wise Ranking 120
16 Problem Tree Chart 122
17 Problem Analysis Chart 125
18 Monitoring and Evaluation in Project Cycle Management 138
19 Butterfly Model of Planning and Evaluation 146

Tables

1 Characteristics of Social Capital 20
2 Models of Community Work 26
3 Difference between Needs Based and Rights Based Approach 31
4 Logical Models Underlying Participatory Strategies 53
5 Putting Rights, Participation and Power into Practice 66
6 Overview of Participatory Approach 76
7 Issue Life Cycle Stages 82
8 Framework for Possible Outcomes of Advocacy 83
9 Indicative Project Planning Matrix-LFA 90
10 Linking PRA to Community Work 93
11 Use of Participatory Methods in Research 127
12 Levels of Monitoring 137
13 Parameters for Participatory Self Monitoring 147
14 Difference between Conventional and Participatory Evaluation 150
15 Engendered Log Frame 157
16 Implementation Monitoring and Outcome Monitoring 158
17 Characteristics of Poor 179
18 Difference between Participatory Poverty Assessment and Other Methods 182
19 Indicative Wealth Ranking Reference Sheet 183

1

Contemporary Social Work and Community Work

The Encyclopedia of Social Work in India (GoI, 1987) brings out that the purpose of social work has always been to assist people in need. Social workers believe in the social betterment or improving the quality of life of the people. Social work looks at itself as being concerned with the underdog—the most vulnerable people in society. As the profession of social work emerged to help people change in relation to a rapidly changing world, the focus of the profession has been on helping people to improve social functioning, that is the manner in which people interact with their environments, the people and the social institutions with which they come in contact.

One of the earliest attempts to describe social work was made by Mary Richmond in her classic 'Social Diagnosis' in 1917. The period from 1920s to early 1950s saw several attempts being made by the American Association of Social Workers, through their various meetings and what are popularly known as the 'Mulford Conferences' to work out a comprehensive definition of social work. A significant step in this direction was the publication of the 'Working Definition of Social Work Practice' in 1958. This working definition identified fundamental areas of commonality in the purpose of social work practice, viz:

- To assist individuals and groups to identify and resolve or minimize problems arising out of disequilibrium between themselves and their environment;

- To identify potential areas of disequilibrium between individuals or groups and the environment in order to prevent the occurrence of disequilibrium; and
- In addition to these curative and preventive aims, to seek out, identify and strengthen the maximum potential in individuals, groups and communities (quoted in Morales and Sheafor, 1989).

The general definition of social work provided by the National Association of Social Workers (NASW) in 1970 has been taken to be one of the most appropriate definitions of Social Work. As per the NASW, 'social work is the professional activity of helping individuals, groups or communities enhance or restore their capacity for social functioning and creating societal conditions favourable to that goal'.

Morales and Sheafor (1989) outline the three purposes of social work as caring, curing and change. Social work is concerned with the well being of the people. In recent times, however, the thrust of social work practice has been to treat people experiencing problems in social functioning. Towards this, techniques like counseling, transactional analysis, family therapy, and behaviour modification etc., have been developed and perfected. Similarly, Social schange has also been an integral part of social work. From reforms in living conditions and services, to impacting social legislation to improve the existing systems, to make them more responsive to human needs has been part of the social change agenda.

Social work is about human beings in their social worlds. Human beings are dynamic in themselves and live in complex worlds. Social work practice therefore, is challenging as it constantly requires dealing with complexity. The process of social work has also thus undergone considerable change; from Perlman's problem-solving model, where social workers were expected to help people identify and overcome problems; to Roger's person-centered model, where the emphasis was on releasing the individuals capacity for self-realisation; to the developmental model propagated by Smalley, wherein social workers tried to help people grow in understanding and skill; to the yet to be universally accepted and recognised critical model, that emphasizes on the transformation of social relations through dialogical, shared relationships.

The initial conceptualizations of the process of social work operated on the premise that each individual has his or her unique needs and people are expected to develop their own means to satisfy most of their needs, with little help from others. If that fails, they should look towards their family and well wishers and only then to the human services. Conservative philosophy places the responsibility of meeting his/her needs squarely on the individual, while the liberal position would like the society to assume more responsibility. Social work has traditionally been predisposed towards the liberal position, though not fully weighted in that direction.

An interesting typology of philosophical views on social welfare was provided by Wilensky and Lebeaux (1965) where they identified two approaches, the residual and the institutional. The residual formulation is based on the premise that the proper sources for meeting a person's needs are the family and the market economy. If these sources fail, the social welfare structure comes into play on a temporary basis to help until the individual or the economic system begins to work properly. The institutional formulation, on the other hand, is based on the perception that social welfare to meet the needs of individuals is one of the frontline functions of the state. This institutional or developmental approach sees social services as basic to the well-being of all people. The state thus assumes the responsibility of the welfare of its people. Welfare states grew out of recognition of this role of the state.

It is accepted that the political philosophy and ideology of the state determines what role the state would have in the lives of the individuals. Different doctrines, be it anarchist or fascist, liberal or social democrat, socialist or communist, differ in their view of society, the beliefs about the proper role of the state and the extent and ways in which a state may intervene in the lives of citizens. On the one end there are doctrines that say that there should be no authority beyond the individual, as each person commands absolutely the conduct of his own life and bows to no other individual or authority. As Rousseau put is, true liberty is found only in obedience to self imposed law and a social contract is a matter of voluntary agreement between free individuals. The state thus becomes subservient to the individual. On the other hand, is the view that the state may treat individual as chattels, to be bought and sold as property of other individuals or as slaves of the state. The individual thus becomes subservient to the state. Between these two extremes, lies the pluralist concept of a welfare state. Such a state allows for diversity and change. It provides equality of opportunity, practices value relativity and conciliation of diverse cultures and groups. The purpose of policy in such a state is to devolve power and give authority to individuals and local groups and encourage self governance. The state actively intervenes in the social and physical environment to change it for the betterment of the people.

Gough I. (1979) defines welfare state as the 'use of state power to modify the reproduction of labour power and to maintain the non-working population in capitalist societies'. The modern welfare state intervenes in this process in several ways:

(i) 'First, the amount of money which people have available to spend on consumption goods is altered via the taxation and social security systems.
(ii) Second, the nature of the use-values which they can purchase may be regulated by the state, as when it controls additives to food or the facilities provided in new housing.
(iii) Third, particular goods and services are subsidized, either for some or for all, such as certain categories of housing or types of food; and
(iv) Fourth, the state directly provides use-values in the form of services such as the National Health Service, free or at a greatly reduced cost'.

From a purely capitalist perspective, the state must try to maintain or create the conditions in which capital accumulation is possible. O'Connor (1973) argues that all state expenditures (in a capitalist state) have a two-fold function: social capital and social expenses. Social capital comprises of two sets of activities, social investment and social consumption. Thus three categories of state expenditures are distinguished:

(i) Social Investment: projects and services that increase the productivity of labour.
(ii) Social Consumption: projects and services that lower the reproduction costs of labour.
(iii) Social Expenses: projects and services that are required to maintain social harmony—to fulfil the state's legitimization function.

The first two are indirectly productive for private capital. Other things being equal, they augment the rate of profit and accumulation in the economy. Social expenses, on the other hand, are not even indirectly productive for capital. They are a necessary but unproductive expense.

In 1982, Mexico declared that it could no longer service debt payments, a declaration that shook the international financial community. The World Bank and the IMF therefore embarked on structural adjustment programmes, to alleviate the worst effects of the heavy debt burden. Through the imposition of policy packages focusing on austerity measures and the rescheduling of loans, the debtor countries were encouraged to continue servicing loans. New loans were conditional on policy changes proposed by the World Bank on a series of macro-economic reforms, known as the stabilization policies and agreed to by the recipient countries. The package of measures typically included deregulation, cuts in public expenditure and bureaucracy, export-led economic growth, elimination of subsidies for food/crops and removal of protection for local farmers and indigenous industries. There was an underlying belief that the free market was the only way to solve economic problems. Studies however, have highlighted the negative impact of the structural adjustment policies. Areas like education and health have experienced the greatest deterioration in provision and concepts like user-fees have impacted on the well-being of women and children.

India flirted with the idea of a socialist welfare state since the very beginning, more so in the early 1950s and late 1970s, when the Community Development Programme, the Minimum Needs Programme and the Integrated Rural Development Programme were launched. However, in-spite of close to seven decades of planned development, a lot is still left to be achieved. More than a quarter of the Indian population continues to live below the poverty line. Disparities in income and living standards are appalling. The rights of a considerable section of the population including the Scheduled Castes and Scheduled Tribes and religious minorities continue to be violated, often by the state. Rights to education, food, livelihood, shelter, life and dignity continue to be pipe-dreams for a majority of the population. Add to this grim scenario is the vigorously pursued reforms agenda that has led to considerable distress, affecting the poor, especially the rural poor the most.

As the former President of India, Mr. K.R. Narayan remarked, 'fifty years into the life of our Republic we find that justice—social, economic and political—remains an unrealized dream for millions of our fellow citizens. The benefits of our economic growth are yet to reach them. We have one of the world's largest reservoir of technical personnel, but also the world's largest number of illiterates, the world's largest middle class, but also the largest number of people below the poverty line, and the largest number of children suffering from malnutrition. Our giant factories arise out of squalor; our satellites shoot up from the midst of the hovels of the poor. Not surprisingly, there is sullen resentment among the masses against their condition erupting often in violent forms in several parts of the country. Tragically, the growth in our economy has not been uniform. It has been accompanied by great regional and social inequalities. Many a social upheaval can be traced to the neglect of the lowest of society, whose discontent moves towards the path of violence' (*Samuel J and Jagadananda, 2003*).

Begining 1991, the economic policy of the country has undergone a radical shift. The processes of globalisation and liberalisation and the structural adjustment programme have changed the nature of Indian state. Privatisation, reduction of subsidies, reduction in social sector allocation have started impacting on the lives of the people. The entry of mutinational corporations, even in the consumer goods sector has spelt the death knell of many a small entrepreneurs in India. A recent report brought out by the Council for Social Development, 'India: Social Development Report (2006) has analysed the social processes, social attitudes and institutions in social development. The report observes that in the post reform period, while there have been improvements in economic growth, increases in foreign exchange, the IT revolution, acceleration in export growth, etc., social exclusion has continued in terms of low agriculture and employment growth, concentration of poverty among the Scheduled Castes and Tribes, and an increase in inequalities and regional disparities. Liberalisation and globalization have not improved social development in general and social exclusion in particular. While examining the major areas of social development in India, the report mentions that the failure to universalize elementary education, wide disparities across gender, regions and social groups are major failures. Poverty, the high cost of good education, and low quality of education are the major factors at the household level for high drop-out rates among the poor. Inequalities in quality education is also a major factor for drop-outs. The report further observes that in the case of women, the dominance of Hindu patriarchal ideology which was prevalent in the colonial period, continued even in the post independence period. Muslims continue to be underprivileged in terms of basic indicators like literacy, income, and consumption expenditure. Regarding children, the report observes that there has been limited success in improving health, nutrition and educational status of children since independence. Discrimination against the girl child is reflected in gender differential death rates, drop out rates, malnutrition and most importantly foeticide. Also, the special problems of several categories of disadvantaged children are not being addressed. These include children of working mothers in need of care, street children, delinquent children, sexually abused children, children of sex workers, children who are victims of trafficking, AIDS orphans, child beggars and other similarly placed children in difficult circumstances.

The near demise of the welfare state thus has implications for the context of social work practice. For the profession of social work, the crisis has been both internal and external (Camilleri P, 1999). The external crisis has been in the relationship between social work and the welfare state. The transformation of the welfare state has seen social work become more marginalized as the ideological framework for services and programmes has shifted significantly to contracting out services through competitive tendering. Social work has been challenged by this new managerialism and finds itself uncomfortably located.

The crisis in social work is manifest at all levels and in all areas of social work activity. 'At the delivery level there have been cuts in social expenditure, increased categorization and targeting of programmes, privatization of many public services, special investigation of welfare recipients, imposition of user fees… along with these changes, changing social needs have increased because of demographic challenges, changing social roles, and increased unemployment and underemployment. The net effect is that it is now impossible to address the economic and social needs of increasing numbers of people in a meaningful way-particularly the poor, the deprived and the most exploited, which include women and unemployed' (Mullaly R.P., 1993). Add to this the adverse effects of globalization and liberalisation, the situation becomes all the more complex and challenging not only for the profession but also for those it seeks to help. New social movements such as feminism, indigenous rights, environmentalism, and rights of the disabled have challenged the discourse of social sciences and demand that they be heard.

The struggle between the conventional and progressive or critical views of society within the discipline of social work, although dealt with, with some measure of success in the west, is yet to be part of the mainstream discourse of social work in India.

The majority of mainstream professional social work practice is influenced by and reflective of 'popular beliefs and attitudes about the nature of the individual, of society, and of the relationship between the two'. Preservation of the status-quo and defining social problems in terms of personal inadequacies that require social work interventions either to help people cope or adjust to existing institutions, are the mainstay of such an approach. On the other hand, the progressive, critical view of society looks at the inadequacies of the present social institutions to meet human needs. The growing gap between the rich and poor, the worsening plight of traditionally disadvantaged groups, and the social control functions of welfare programmes and social work practice are presented as proof that the present set of social arrangements does not work for large numbers of people (See also Mullaly R.P., 1993).

It is commonly agreed that emancipatory social work began with the development of radical critiques in the 1970s with writers such as Bailey and Brake (1975, 1980) and Leonard (1975). Maurice Moreau (1979) is credited with the initial naming of structural social work although extensive development of the approach has been carried out by Mullaly (1993). Radical and structural models of social work were criticized for their lack of sensitivity towards gender dimensions. Feminist social work models, that were better at developing the links between analysis and practice, and between personal and political experience, therefore started emerging. The structural, radical and feminist models of social work practice, developed to date are mostly based on the principle that the aim of social work should be to empower less powerful people or groups. This, of course, assumes that the possession of power acts as the great divide in our social organization, and that people generally either belong mutually exclusively to one of two groups: powerful or powerless, advantaged or disadvantaged, oppressor or oppressed, exploiter or exploited. The division usually occurs across gender, class, cultural or racial lines (Fook J. & Pease B, 1999).

The fact is that if social work truly believes in the values and ideals it espouses, then it cannot try and maintain a social order that contradicts and violates many of these same values and ideals.

Structural social work arose as a response to such ideas. In structural social work, the major sources of social problems are described as being located in the way our society is structured; and because social problems are rooted in our social structures, then the structures must be changed and not the individual, the family or the subculture adversely affected by social problems. Alongwith structural social work there has arisen a new paradigm in social work, that of critical social work. The critical social work approach emphasizes a commitment to standing alongside oppressed and impoverished populations; the importance of dialogical relations between workers and service users; the role of social, economic and political systems in shaping individual experiences and social relationships, including interactions within the practice context; and a commitment to the 'study of change, the move towards change' and the provocation of change. Critical practice is oriented towards the transformation of processes and structures that perpetuate domination and exploitation (See Healy K, 2001). Critical social work refers to a broad range of practice theories that share the following orientations:

- A recognition that large scale social processes, particularly those associated with class, race and gender, contribute fundamentally to the personal and social issues social workers encounter in their practice;
- The adoption of a self-reflexive and critical stance to the often contradictory effects of social work practice and social policies;
- A commitment to co-participatory rather than authoritarian practice relations. This involves workers and service users, as well as academic practitioners and service users as co-participants engaged with, but still distinct from, one another; and
- Working with and for oppressed populations to achieve social transformation.

The core mission of critical social work is to promote social justice through social work practice and policy making. To this end, critical social workers have pursued practice theories that prioritise social structural analyses and promote collaborative approaches to action. A critical approach to practice calls for reflection on action, and the use of critical questions to keep focus:

- How is your practice influenced by an anti-discriminatory analysis?
- In what ways are dominant ideas and national policy changes impacting on the diverse lives of the people?
- What evidence is there that your practice contributes to change for social justice and environmental justice?
- How can you extend collective action beyond the boundaries of community to build national, international and global alliances?

Critical practice theorists are adept at responding to challenges from outside their tradition; from the proponents of conservatism, economic rationalism and, more recently managerialism. Substantial structural changes over the past few decades, including the rise of globalisation and market driven approaches to the management of human services, however, already threaten the continuation of critical practice traditions in social work (Healy K, 2001).

Social work itself has been drawn into the latest fashions and fads of government or donor agenda, as that is where the money is. Instead of developing and maintaining a clear analysis of society and societal issues, to inform action, social work seems to be overwhelmingly concerned with developing and sharpening skills. What is required is critical and analytical thinking about the theory and politics of community work; good quality literature to help students develop their critical faculties, so that they are able to think through the implications of their work. As Craig (2004) puts it, "I think that practice is dominated by the policy and political context rather than creating it".

Community and Community Work

Before 1910 there was little social science literature concerning 'community' and it was only around 1915 that the first clear sociological definition emerged. Hillary (1955) in his 'Definitions of Community' had listed approximately ninety-four definitions of community, leading commentators to write it off as a 'non-concept' and a confusing terminology. C.J. Galpin coined the term in relation to delineating rural communities in terms of the trade and service areas surrounding a central village (Harper & Dunham 1959). The term community has been explored in three different ways: place, interest and communion. A territorial or place community can be seen as where people have something in common, and this shared element is understood geographically. Another way this has been understood is in terms of a 'locality'. In interest or 'elective' communities people share a common characteristic other than place. They are linked together by factors such as religious belief, sexual orientation, occupation or ethnic origin. In this way we may talk about the 'gay community', the 'Catholic community' or the 'Chinese community'. In its weakest form we can approach community as a sense of attachment to a place, group or idea (in other words, whether there is a 'spirit of community'). In its strongest form 'communion' entails a profound meeting or encounter—not just with other people, but also with God and creation like the Christian communion or Muslim community or *Ummah* (http://www.infed.org/community).

Clarke (1973) in his article on 'The Concept of Community: A Re-examination' has examined the concept of community as locality, as a social activity, as social structure and as a sentiment. He has pointed out that locality is one of the fundamental bases of a community and has examined the effect of physical environment on social relationships. Quoting Pahl's doctrine of architectural determinism, he points out that 'there has remained an extraordinarily tenacious belief that community is a phenomenon that can be physically engineered'. However, it is important to note as White (1974) proposes, that all 'evidence suggests that there are certain fairly well defined limits of size, population and density within which neighbourliness is easily fostered, and outside which the community tends to disintegrate'. While elaborating on community as a social activity, Clarke draws heavily on Frankenberg's study, Village on the Border (1957). Frankenberg has argued that a detailed description and analysis of 'dramatic occurrences' (special events, ceremonials or customs) can reveal a great deal about communal life. Such dramatic occurrences like ceremonials surrounding individual and family life crises—such as christenings, weddings and funerals, reactions to individual tragedies like fire, flood and accidents, perennial occurrences like Christmas, Easter, bank holidays, holidays in general, elections and meetings and occasional celebrations such as Coronations and parades etc. reveal a great deal about the community. This approach provides a more penetrating understanding of what is actually happening within the group, especially in regard to group attitudes and motives. The question is, to what extent these occasions really express the sentiment of the group, or do such occasions create an artificial set of conditions that may be different from how the group normally behaves.

Additionally, when we consider community as social structure, we examine the social structure of the group, with emphasis on the study of institutions and of the concepts of role, status and social class. Community to the structuralists appears more as a local social system, i.e., a social network as a meaningful arena for social relationships. Some argue that any perceptive study of community must take into account not only the usual pattern of social behaviour as it appears outwardly, but the attitudes of people towards the normative order as a whole. MacIver (1961) mentions that 'life is essentially and always communal life. Every living thing is born into community and owes its life to community'. Simpson (1937) points out that 'community is no circumscribed sphere of social life, but rather the very life blood of social life. Community is not simply economic, nor simply political, nor simply territorial, nor simply visceral. Nor is it all these special elements added together. Ultimately it is a complex of conditioned emotions which the individual feels towards the surrounding world and his fellows...It is to human beings and their feelings, sentiments, reactions that all look for the fundamental roots of community'.

The two fundamental communal elements of any social system are a sense of solidarity and a sense of significance (Clarke,

1973). This solidarity is similar to what has been referred to as 'we-feeling', a feeling that leads men to identify themselves with others, so that when they say 'we' there is no thought of division. Solidarity is the most commonly accepted ingredient of community and is represented by social unity, togetherness, social cohesion, or a sense of belonging. It encompasses all those sentiments, which draw people together (sympathy, courtesy, gratitude, trust etc). The second element, is that of a sense of significance, very similar to the term 'role feeling', i.e., a sense of place or station, experienced by group members, so that each person feels he has a role to play and his own function to fulfil in the reciprocal exchanges of the social scene (MacIver & Page, 1961). Significance would also include a sense of achievement or fulfilment, all contributing to the larger whole. Another element is that of a sense of security—a dependence of the individual on the community as a necessary condition of his own life. This includes both physical as well as psychological dependency on the community for sustenance and satisfaction of material needs etc.

Kinglsey Davis (1961) has defined community as 'the smallest territorial group that can embrace all aspects of human life... It is the smallest local group that can be and often is a complete society'. But, as Davis points out, the modern community cannot be understood in terms of itself alone. Each segment may be more closely linked with similar segments in other communities than with dissimilar elements in the same community. We must therefore take into account different groups, networks and communities-of-interest interconnected in various ways and to varying degrees and occupying varying and overlapping territories. Often they are more strongly related to similar groups, networks and communities-of-interest outside the area than to others within it.

What then do we think of when we speak of 'community'? Is it simply a group of people living in the same geographic area? Is it a group of people who share common values, ideas, and beliefs about the world? Community is often defined as a group of people with a shared locality and a shared set of common values. However, what is missing is a sense of the linkages, the interrelationships,

An ideal community should furnish to its human constituents :

* *Order or security of life and property through the medium of an efficient government.*
* *Economic well-being or security of income through an efficient system of productive industry.*
* *Physical well-being, or health and sanitation through public health agencies.*
* *Constructive use of leisure time, or recreation though public health agencies.*
* *Ethical standards or a system of morality supported by the organized community.*
* *Intellectual diffusion or education through free and public institutions within the reach of all.*
* *Free avenues of expression, or means by which all the elements of the community might freely express themselves; free newspapers and public forums.*
* *Democratic forms of organization, or community-wide organization through which the entire community might express its thought and see that its will is done.*
* *Spiritual motivation or religious associations, which might diffuse throughout all forms of community organization the religious or spiritual motive.*

Source: Lindeman (1921)

between community members that serve to identify individuals as part of a community and allow others to recognize individuals as part of a community. The strength of the linkages in the social network is the defining aspect of a strong community. A community is representative of the relationships between people and their interaction on an everyday basis. People need to have the capacity to come together, share, relate, and talk about their values and interests. Social networks are the means by which individual community members interrelate and create a sense of community. They are the interpersonal connections that people participate in as they carry out day-to-day activities. The capacity to share values and interests allows a community to develop strong bonds and a high level of trust among individuals.

Strong community affiliation creates a sense of security; a sense of belonging that reaffirms our existence as social beings. A strong community allows for diversity, while incorporating that diversity into its whole. A strong, effective community creates a sense of ownership and responsibility for the entire group that goes beyond individual self-interest. The community provides '...individuals with a web of trust and social support that is desperately needed in this transient, swiftly changing society' (Gardner, J.W. 1995). When social networks produce lasting ties, linkages, trust, and a collection of shared values, the survival of the community becomes more important than individual self-interest or gain. Community members realize that their own personal well-being is closely linked to the health of the community as a whole. When members of the community from different positions, roles, and cultures come together to discuss and debate issues of importance to the community then social networks are strengthened. However, many communities do not possess strong social networks. Communities, which lack strong social networks, or lack the means to use their existing social networks, are at a disadvantage when faced with external conditions that require community action and community renewal (See also, Brett Lane & Diane Dorfman, 1997). This emphasis on affiliation, interaction and social networks has found mention in a new concept, that of social capital.

Putnam (1995) has defined 'social capital' as the features of social organization, such as networks, norms and social trust that facilitate coordination and cooperation for mutual benefit. Social capital can comprise both horizontal relationships of social support, between members of a community, family or household and vertical relationships between communities and institutions, such as government bodies. Alternatively, social capital can be divided into bonding and bridging capital, where bonding capital refers to social cohesion within the group structure, and bridging capital refers to the type that links or cuts across different communities and groups (Narayan, 1999). Any analysis of community negotiating strategies for development needs to consider all these aspects of social capital as this will affect whether a community can act as a cohesive unit (bonding), whether it can access groups with power or resources than itself (bridging), whether it is operating within a hierarchical system (vertical) and whether it has links with other community organizations (horizontal).

An alternative construct of social capital focuses upon the structural and cognitive components. Krishna and Shrader (2000) describe structural social capital as including 'the composition and practices of local level institutions, both formal and informal, that serve as instruments of community development'. Structural social capital is built through horizontal organizations and networks that have collective and transparent decision making processes, accountable leaders, and practices of collective action and mutual responsibility. Structural social capital then refers to the networks, linkages and practices within and between communities. In contrast, cognitive social capital refers to the values, beliefs, attitudes, social norms and behaviour that exist within communities, such as social trust and norms, solidarity and reciprocity. While cognitive elements predispose people towards mutually beneficial collective action, structural elements of social capital facilitate such action. Both structural and cognitive dimensions matter and they must be combined to represent the aggregate potential for mutually beneficial collective action that exists within any community.

Social capital currently refers to the 'stocks of social trust, norms, and networks that people can draw upon to solve common problems' (Putnam, R. 1993a). Contemporary use of the term social capital originates in the work of Pierre Bourdieu and James Coleman in the 1970's. The recent work of Putnam (1993a) and Fukuyama (1995) have extended the concept of social capital to apply not only to individuals but also to groups, communities, and even nations. This transition allows them to claim that a community, rather than an individual has a certain amount of social capital. Communities 'build' social capital through the development of active relationships, democratic participation, and the strengthening of community ownership and trust.

Social capital is a measurement of the levels of social trust and active relationships present in the social networks of a community. Strong social networks and high levels of active relationships between individuals from different roles in the community tend to '...foster sturdy norms of generalized reciprocity and encourage the emergence of social trust' (Putnam, 1995). Community members expect and understand that important community issues are going to be dealt with by all members of the community and that multiple viewpoints will be expressed and valued. It becomes normal for diverse community members and institutions to engage in dialogue and debate about issues that affect the entire community. Community members also trust community leaders and peers to include diverse members and views when decisions affecting the entire community are being made.

Cortes (1993) describes social capital as a 'measure of how much collaborative time and energy people have for each other, how much time parents have for their children, how much attention neighbors will give to each other's families, what kind of relationships people in congregations have with each other,...and the quality of many other potential webs of relationships in a community'. Social capital is a way to look at all relationships in a community. It enables us to measure how strong the passive relationships such as the parent/child relationship are, and how strong the active relationships between diverse members of the community are. In essence, social capital is expressive of the strength of the entire social network of a community. It is the strength of these social networks, the stock of social capital that truly defines a community and increases the capacity of the community to deal with internal and external problems or changes. In the words of Cortes 'social capital implies a richness and robustness of relationships among people that the members of a community are willing and eager to invest in one another'.

Putnam in his *Bowling Alone: The collapse and revival of American community* articulates the importance of social capital. 'First, social capital allows citizens to resolve collective problems more easily... People often might be better off if they cooperate, with each doing her share. But each individual benefits more by shirking their responsibility, hoping that others will do the work for her.... [Resolving this dilemma is] best served by an institutional mechanism with the power to ensure compliance with the collectively desirable behaviour. Social norms and the networks that enforce them provide such a mechanism.

Second, social capital greases the wheels that allow communities to advance smoothly. Where people are trusting and trustworthy, and where they are subject to repeated interactions with fellow citizens, everyday business and social transactions are less costly....

A third way is which social capital improves our lot is by widening our awareness of the many ways in which our fates are linked. People who have active and trusting connections to others—whether family members, friends, or fellow bowlers—develop or maintain character traits that are good for the rest of society. Joiners become more tolerant, less cynical, and more empathetic to the misfortunes of others. When people lack connection to others, they are unable to test the veracity of their own views, whether in the give or take of casual conversation or in more formal deliberation. Without such an opportunity, people are more likely to be swayed by their worse impulses....

The networks that constitute social capital also serve as conduits for the flow of helpful information that facilitates achieving our goals.... Social capital also operates through psychological and biological processes to improve individual's lives. Mounting evidence suggests that people whose lives are rich in social capital cope better with traumas and fight illness more effectively. ... Community connectedness is not just about warm fuzzy tales of civic triumph. In measurable and well-documented ways, social capital makes an enormous difference to our lives' (2000).

The development of social capital requires adequate levels of five basic attributes.

- *Interest*: People show attention to what is going on outside their immediate circle, can recognise others' needs and express respect for diversity of views and customs.
- *Participation*: There is engagement and interest in working collectively for common purposes.
- *Trust in people*: People are willing to trust others, whether familiar or unfamiliar.
- *Trust in institutions*: People are prepared to work for change within the democratic process of government, and through the legal system.

- *Capacity to resolve conflict civilly*: People feel comfortable exploring and accepting the different and new (Eva Cox, 2002).

The table given below, deleneates the characteristics of high and low level social capital:

Table 1: Characteristics of Social Work

Characteristics of high level social capital	*Characteristics of low level social capital*
• Accepted mechanisms used for conflict resolution between different interest groups. • Wide variety of community activities (*e.g.* in various clubs, sports, crafts, the arts, plus informal use of public space for activities). • Vitality of civic organisations and activities (new members, new people participating, long term commitment). • High joint use of public spaces by diverse groups (young and old, long term and more recent residents, different activities accepted, *e.g.* dog walking, football, children playing. • Observable friendly interactions in public places, streets, shops, etc., such as conversations, smiles, courtesy and eye contact. • Helpfulness to strangers, responsiveness to needs of others in public spaces. • Honesty (*e.g.* lost articles handed in; cars safely left unlocked, goods left in cars). • Inclusive community activities (*e.g.* reconciliation meetings, Land Care).	• Obvious levels of overt conflict without resolution (demonstrations and campaigns which involve violent and abusive interactions, gangs, street violence). • Easy classification of unfamiliar people as "others", a sense that "it's their problem". • Obvious levels of anger in particular groups based on perceptions of unfairness or feeling threatened which could be expressed in high levels of litigation against local institutions such as local government, public complaints in newspapers, complaints to official ombudsmen or other arbiters, angry letters, stories in media, etc.). • Hostility toward, or scapegoating of, particular groups (*e.g.* too many young people on the streets. • Lack of civic pride (littering, vandalism, low maintenance of public spaces). • Lack of interest in civic initiatives (low attendance at public meetings, low voter turnout for local elections, few nominations for political office).

(*Contd.*)

(Contd.)

Characteristics of high level social capital	*Characteristics of low level social capital*
• Feeling safe (children going to school, shops and parks on their own, people walking freely in streets at night, few notices up about theft and security, unlocked entrances, accessible public toilets). • Acceptance of new groups of residents and different populations into existing formal and informal groups (integration of different layers of migration, signs of inclusive networks, cross group friendships, respect for difference).	• Little networking at local level with neighbours, few local shops, few connections with others and low use of public places and streets. • Failure of community activities due to lack of support and participation. • High levels of physical security (*e.g.*, bars, alarms, security officers, gated communities), exaggerated fear of crime. • Low levels of use of public spaces, perceived high risks (in parks, streets, public transport, fear of crime out of proportion to actual levels). • High levels of street offences, harmful and risky behaviours (drinking, public order flouting, hassling pedestrians, begging, public hovering). • High levels of mistrust of any form of development or change, particularly rejection of public amenities, protecting local real estate, police complaints about loitering. • Highly stratified communities with little or no mixing of subgroups.

Source: Eva Cox, 2002

The World Bank affirms the utility of social capital; that there is evidence that schools are more effective when parents and local citizens are actively involved. 'Teachers are more committed, students achieve higher test scores, and better use is made of school facilities in those communities where parents and citizens take an active interest in children's educational well-being'. They also indicate some negative impacts, for example, when disgruntled local elites joined together to close health clinics in Uttar Pradesh. Child mortality rates soared as a result (www.worldbank.org/poverty/scapital/whatsc.htm).

Mulgan G. (1997) asserts that at the core of the idea of community are three basic principles. 'The first is the simple recognition of people's social nature, and one might add, of the sociability, sense of fairness, sympathy and duty'. This softer value—social capital that enables people to work together, to trust each other, to commit to common causes—has proved absolutely critical to societal success, whether in narrow economic terms or in terms of well-being. The second principle is about scale. Community is deliberately a different word from society. It may refer to neighbourhoods or workplaces, but to be meaningful, it must imply membership in a human–scale collective: a scale at which it is possible to encounter people face to face.... (and) to nurture human-scale structures within which people can feel at home. The third principle is the reaffirmation of ethics—the recognition that any viable politics needs to be prepared to make judgments about behaviour and about what types of behaviour work against the common interest and against the interest of future generations. Without a strong sense of personal ethics, societies require an unacceptable level of policing and contracts; and without a strong sense of personal responsibility it is inevitable that costs will be shunted out on the natural environment and on to the future generations.

Community Organisation

Let us briefly examine what we mean by community organization and how does it figure in the discourse of social work. Lindeman (1926) defined community organization as 'those phases of social organization, which constitute a conscious effort on the part of a community to control its affairs democratically, and to secure the highest services from its specialists, organizations, agencies, and the institutions by means of recognized interrelations'. Ross (1955) saw community organization as 'a process by which a community identifies its needs or objectives, orders (or ranks) these needs or objectives, develops the confidence and the will to work at these needs or objectives, finds the resources (internal and/or external) to deal with these needs or objectives, takes action in respect to them, and in so doing extends and develops co-operative and collaborative attitudes and practices in the community'. For him community organization seems to have two broad aims, the achievement of certain community identified goals; and the development of co-operative and collaborative attitudes and practices. The Younghusband Report (1959) on social work was a significant turning point. It specifically drew on the north American division of social work into case work, group work and community organization, describing the latter as 'primarily aimed at helping people within a local community to identify social needs, to consider the most effective ways of meeting these and to set about doing so, in so far as their available resources permit'. Community work was taken as 'helping local people to decide, plan and take action to meet their own needs with the help of available outside resources; helping local services to become more effective, usable and accessible to those whose needs they are trying to meet; taking account of the interrelation between different services in planning for people; and forecasting necessary adoptions to meet new social needs in constantly changing circumstances' (Gulbenkian 1968).

David Thomas in a report sponsored by the Calouste Gulbenkian Foundation pointed out that community work had three major aspects:

'First, to help people take action on specific issues of importance to them. These issues will almost invariably involve the influence of resources, either those held, for example, by local authorities, or to be found within communities themselves... referred to as the distributive aspect of community work. It is equivalent to the conventional category of 'product goals' familiar in community work literature. Influence on the distribution of resources will be terminal goals for the people involved, but (I have argued) that we should see them also as instrumental in contributing towards.

Secondly, the development of political responsibility; and
Thirdly, that of communal coherence'. (Thomas, 1983)

In the late 1960s there was some exploration of different models of participation and their relationship to community development. Concepts like popular participation and community participation gained currency, mostly due to their adoption by various international agencies, notably of the United Nations. As Midgley *et al.* (1986) have noted, the notion of popular participation and that of community participation were interlinked. The former was concerned with broad issues of social development and the creation of opportunities for the involvement of people in the political, economic and social life of a nation, 'the latter connotes the direct involvement of ordinary people in local affairs'.

Most definitions of community work have considered it as 'being concerned to enable people to develop collective responses to shared needs, whether these needs relate directly to the concerns of social service departments, such as community care or child care needs, or whether these community needs effectively require responses from one or more different agencies, crossing departmental and sectoral boundaries' (Mayo, M. 1994).

Community work has taken on a range of meanings. It has been associated with policies from both right and left. The political debates of the 1960s shaped the way community work was viewed. Instead of seeking to help deprived communities to improve their social and environmental circumstances, the new community work activists urged that people take direct political action to demand changes and improvements' (Midgley et al. 1986). Twelvetrees has categorized the different approaches to community work in terms of 'professional' community work, in contrast with 'radical' community work, the latter drawing upon neo-Marxist and feminist analyses of society (Mayo, M. 1994).

He defines the 'professional' approach in terms of professional concerns to promote self-help, and to improve the effectiveness and appropriateness of service delivery, within the wider framework of existing social relations. Alternatively the 'radical' approach emphasizes the potential contribution of community work to shifting the framework of existing social relations, empowering the powerless to question the causes of their deprivation, and to challenge the sources of their oppression, with a focus upon anti-racist and anti-sexist work' (Twelvetrees, 1991)

Rothman identified three distinct types of community organizing: Locality Development, Social Action and Social Planning (Rothman, J. 1968). Locality development for Rothman typifies the methods of work with community groups used by early settlement houses and in 'colonial' community development work. A major focus is on the process of community building. Working with a broad, representative cross section of the community, workers attempt to achieve change objectives by enabling the community to establish consensus via the identification of common interests. Leadership development and the education of the participants are important elements in the process. In this approach great store is set by the values of both participation and leadership.

Social action is employed by groups and organizations, which seek to alter institutional policies or to make changes in the distribution of power. Civil rights groups and social movements are examples. Participation is the value most clearly articulated by those who use this approach. Both leadership and expertise may be challenged as the symbolic 'enemies of the people'.

Social planning is the method of community organization where effort is focused primarily on task goals and issues of resource allocation. Whereas the initial emphasis of this approach was on the co-ordination of social services, its attention has expanded to include programme development and planning in all major social welfare institutions. Heavy reliance is placed on rational problem solving and the use of technical methods such as research and systems analysis. Expertise is the cherished value in this approach, although leadership is accorded importance as well.

Table 2: Models of Community Work Practice

Dimensions	*Locality Development*	*Social Planning*	*Social Action*
Goals	Self help and community integration	Problem solving of substantive community problems	Shifting power and resources
Assumptions	Community lacks viable relationships and democratic problem solving capacity	Substantial social problems exist, *e.g.*, unemployment, illiteracy	Disadvantaged populations experience injustice, inequality and deprivation
Basic Change Strategy	Broad cross-section of community in determining and solving problems	Fact-gathering and rational decision making on most effective course of action	Crystallise issue and organize people to take action against enemy targets
Characteristic methods	Improve community relations among different groups, build consensus	Build consensus or induce conflict confrontation,	Induce conflict through direct action and negotiation
Agency types	Settlement houses, peace corps, consumer associations	Welfare councils, planning bodies	Social movement groups

Source: Rothman (1968).

The Study Group Report 'Community Work and Social Change' (known popularly as the Gulbenkian Foundation Report, 1968) has characterized the nature and purpose of community work as 'consist(ing) of work with groups of local people who have come into existence because they want to change something or do something that concerns them. Community work also embraces attempts to relate the activities of social agencies more closely to the needs of the people they serve. This may include inter-agency cooperation, study and planning, as well as similar action over wider geographical areas or aspects of social policy'. It also identified three main inter-related levels of community work:

- Grassroots or neighbourhood work (working with local individuals, families and community groups);
- Local agency and inter-agency work (working with local umbrella organizations, federations and other local—authority wide organizations, together with local statutory and voluntary organizations); and
- Regional and national community planning work (working on economic development issues which span wider than the local boundaries).

Thomas (1983) isolated main strands or approaches in his study of community work in the early 1980s:

Community action focuses on the organisation of those adversely affected by the decisions, or non-decisions, of public and private bodies and by more general structural characteristics of society. The strategy aims to promote collective action to challenge existing socio-political and economic structures and processes, to explore and explain the power realities of people's situations and through this twin pronged approach, develop both critical perspectives of the status quo and alternative bases of power and action.

Community development emphasises self-help, mutual support, the building up of neighbourhood integration, the development of neighbourhood capacities for problem solving and self-representation, and the promotion of collective action to bring a community's preferences to the attention of political decision-makers.

Social planning is concerned with the assessment of community needs and problems and the systematic planning of strategies for meeting them. Social planning comprises the analysis of social conditions, social policies and agency services; the setting of goals and priorities; the design of service programmes and the mobilisation of appropriate resources; and the implementation and evaluation of services and programmes.

Community organisation involves the collaboration of separate community or welfare agencies with or without the additional participation of statutory authorities, in the promotion of joint initiatives. Service extension is a strategy which seeks to extend agency operations and services by making them more relevant and accessible. This includes extending services into the community, giving these services and the staff who are responsible for them, a physical presence in a neighbourhood.

Methods of community work can be seen in terms of two ends of a continuum—the directive/non-directive. A non-directive approach is one where 'decision and action lie with the members of the group themselves. The characteristics are self-determination, a process where the group identifies its own needs, makes it own plans and works largely by self-help to their realization. The community worker is an enabler in this process, not the director or manager'. On the other hand is the directive approach 'where the main decisions are taken by the official or leader or council and programmes and policies are worked out on this basis. Imposition rather than self-determination is the characteristic and active participation may be limited to a small committee or inner official group' (Batten, 1967*)*. Community workers often need to carry out tasks that would involve some or a combination of the following:

- Making contact with the community, the individuals, groups and organisations in the community;
- Developing a community profile, assessing community resources and needs;
- Developing a strategic analysis, with aims, objectives and targets etc;
- Facilitating the establishment of groups, their maintenance and effective development;
- Working productively with conflict, within and between groups and organizations;
- Collaborating, networking, and negotiating with other agencies and professions;
- Relating effectively to policy making and implementation, including local leadership and governance structures;
- Managing resources, including staff time and budgets;
- Monitoring and evaluating progress; and
- Withdrawing from groups/community.

Characteristically social work has been 'provider-led', that is the providers have shaped it, not the people for whom it is intended (*See also Croft & Beresford, 1994*). Problems like paternalism, unequal relationship between provider and beneficiary, institutionalization, inadequate safeguards for the rights of the service users and abuse etc., crop up in such a provider led approach. More critical issues like those of gender, race, and class also tend to get less importance in this approach.

Social work has, from the beginning, emphasized on the needs of the people. The International Federation of Social Workers, an organization comprising a large professional membership, including the National Association of Social Workers (NASW) has identified the values and code of ethical behaviours that are appropriate for all social workers (Morales and Sheafor, 1989). The preamble to the code states that 'social work originates from humanitarian ideals and democratic philosophy and has universal application to meet human needs arising from personal-societal interactions and to develop human potential'. Within the profession of social work, there has been an overwhelming emphasis on fulfilling people's needs. In the last decade however, human rights-based approaches have gained more attention in the development discourse. With the coming into force of the International Bill of Rights which comprises the Universal Declaration of Human Rights, and the consequent International Covenant on Economic, Social and Cultural Rights (ICESCR) and the International Covenant on Civil and Political Rights (ICCPR), the focus has been more on a rights based approach to development. Other central human rights documents are the Convention on the Rights of the Child (CRC), Convention on the Elimination of All Forms of Discrimination Against Women (CEDAW) and the International Convention on the Elimination of All Forms of Racial Discrimination (CERD). In addition, norms, standards and principles have been developed by a variety of international processes and fora. These provide the framework within which substantial development activity takes place and subsequently has implications for social work practice too.

A rights-based approach to development is a conceptual framework for the process of human development that is normatively based on international human rights standards and operationally directed to promoting and protecting human rights. Essentially, a rights-based approach integrates the norms, standards and principles of the international human rights system into the plans, policies and processes of development. The norms and standards are those contained in the wealth of international treaties and declarations (http://www.unhchr.ch). A rights-based approach to development describes situations not simply in terms of human needs, or of development requirements, but in terms of society's obligations to respond to the inalienable rights of individuals, empowers people to demand justice as a right, not a charity, and gives communities a moral basis from which to claim international assistance when needed.

Regarding socio-economic development as part of the human rights agenda is not new. It dates back to when the authors of the Universal Declaration of Human Rights (1948) articulated economic, social, cultural, civil and political human rights in a single document. A rights-based approach holds that a person for whom a number of human rights remain unfulfilled—such as the right to food, health, education, information, participation, etc.—is a poor person. Poverty is thus *more* than lack of resources—it is the manifestation of exclusion and powerlessness. In this context, the realisation of human rights and the process of development are not distinct. On the contrary, development becomes a sub-set of the process of fulfilling human rights. In fact, development itself is recognised as a human right.

The rights-based definition of development in article 1 of the Declaration on the Right to Development sees it as a comprehensive economic, social, cultural and political process. Its object is the constant improvement of the well-being of the entire population and of all individuals, on the basis of their active, free and meaningful participation in development and in the fair distribution of the resulting benefits. The human rights approach to development is therefore integrated and multidisciplinary.

There are some fundamental differences in the earlier needs based approach and the rights based approach.

Table 3: Difference between Needs Based and Rights Based Approach

Needs Approach	*Human Rights Approach*
Works toward outcome goals	Work towards outcome and process goals
Recognises needs as valid claims	Recognises that rights always implies obligations of the state
Empowerment is not necessary to meet all needs	Recognises that rights can only be realised with empowerment
Accepts charity as the driving motivation for meeting needs	Regards charity as an insufficient motivation for meeting needs
Focuses on manifestations of problems and immediate causes of problems	Focuses on structural causes of problems, as well as manifestations and immediate causes of problems
Focuses on the social context with little emphasis on policy	Focuses on social, economic, cultural, civil and political context and is policy-oriented

Developed by Ljungman, Cecila M., 2005

As the above table illustrates, under the rights based approach, the focus of the work is towards outcome and process goals. This approach also takes into consideration that whenever we mention rights, it would always imply the obligations of the state and other duty-bearers as well. The rights approach recognises that rights can only be realized through a process of empowerment and charity is not a sufficient motivation to meet the needs of people. Rather, it focuses on understanding the structural causes of problems as well as their manifestations and immediate causes of problems. The approach focuses on social, economic, cultural, civil and political context and is policy oriented. In contrast, the earlier need based approach appears to be almost diametrically opposite to the rights based approach. While engaged in a rights based practice, it is important that we look at issues not as problems, but as violations of human rights. Rights based practice seeks to address gaps and violations of rights, strengthen structures and mechanisms, *e.g.* policy change, legislation development, institution building; and strengthen communities and civil society's capacity to support rights.

As different sectors of civil society grapple with increasing challenges of poverty, exclusion, and violence, there is a growing trend to combine concepts and experiences from the fields of human rights and participatory development into their programmes. Interest in shifting to a 'rights-based approach' to development has intensified in recent years. International development agencies have increasingly begun to frame their work in terms of rights. Similarly, human rights organisations have been exploring concepts and strategies of participation and how to apply them to their work.

From an analysis of the differences between approaches, conducted by Celestine Nyamu-Musembi & Andrea Cornwall (2004), it is possible to identify four ways in which human rights are deployed in rights-based approaches to development:

- As a set of normative principles to guide the way in which development is done;
- As a set of instruments with which to develop assessments, checklists and indicators against which interventions might be judged;
- As a component to be integrated into programming; and
- As the underlying justification for interventions aimed at strengthening institutions.

As they point out 'each of these four dimensions has its strengths but also limitations and therefore pursuing any one on its own is likely to prove inadequate. For instance, regarding the rights-based approach as a broad set of principles defining an overarching approach to development can mean that the approach simply serves as a new way of repackaging interventions, one that does not need to refer to anything more than good intentions. At the same time reducing the rights-based approach to a set of instruments (*e.g.* a narrow set of international conventions) or a checklist to be ticked off runs the risk of making it yet another 'layer' to be considered, and something to which only tokenistic lip-service may be given. This also poses the additional risk of establishing a comfort zone within the bounds of well established rights rather than allowing for a broader interpretation of human rights that would encompass much of that development'.

There is agreement on the normative framework for a rights based approach. The international instruments and the authoritative interpretations of the human rights treaty bodies offer a normative roadmap for development to policy makers and practitioners that pursue a rights-based approach. There are six key principles that are derived from the human rights instruments. These are:

- Universalism and inalienability
- Equality and non-discrimination
- Indivisibility and interdependence of human rights
- Participation and Inclusion
- Accountability
- Rule of law

The principle of the universality of human rights implies that every human person, woman, man or child is entitled to enjoy his or her rights simply by virtue of being human. The rights are inalienable in that they cannot be taken away from someone or voluntarily given up. The principle of equality and non-discrimination envisages that all persons within a society enjoy equal access to the available goods and services that are necessary to fulfil basic human needs. The principle of indivisibility and inter-dependence of rights recognises that the enjoyment of one right is indivisibly interrelated to the enjoyment of other rights because all rights are inter-dependent. The inter-dependence of rights is a reflection of the multi-dimensional character of well-being. The principle of non-retrogression states that the prioritisation of some rights must not deliberately be at the expense of the level of realisation of other rights. Thus care must be taken to ensure that other rights maintain at least their initial level of realisation. Law must protect human rights. The rule of law entails that disputes should be solved through adjudication by competent, impartial and independent processes. Aggrieved rights-holders require access to the judicial machinery to invoke their rights to institute legal proceedings for appropriate redress. The principle of accountability is derived from the fact that rights implies duties and duties demand accountability. To demand the accountability of policy-makers and other actors whose actions impact on the rights of people, contributes to moving development from the realm of charity to that of obligation, making it easier to monitor progress. This is arguably the most important value-addition of a rights-based approach. Accountability requires that the government, as the legal and principle duty bearer:

- Accepts responsibility for the impact it has on people's lives;
* Co-operates by providing information, undertaking transparent processes and hearing people's views; and
* Responds adequately to those views (UNDP, 2000).

Accountability requires conditions for transparency and avenues for challenging and seeking redress for decisions or actions negatively affecting rights. While it is up to duty-bearers to determine the appropriate mechanisms of accountability themselves, all mechanisms must be accessible, transparent and effective (OHCHR, 2002).

The principle of participation—which is recognised as a right in itself—means that every person and all peoples are entitled to participate in, contribute to, and enjoy civil, economic, social and political development. It also means that all people are entitled to participate in society to the maximum of their potential. This, in turn, necessitates taking steps to facilitate participation, including the provision of supportive environments to enable people to develop and express their full potential and creativity.

Participation is an entitlement guaranteed by international law and thus an imperative in the rights framework. In effect, as much importance is attached to the processes of achieving goals, as it is to the goals themselves. A rights-based strategy, therefore, must aim for free, active and meaningful participation of targeted communities. 'Free' means participation that is not imposed. A community could therefore, in theory, decide to have their views represented by someone or could decide to entrust technicians to make specific technical choices for a project. 'Active' requires that the participation process is going somewhere; and 'meaningful' participation entails that it is consequential for goals achieved (Human Rights Council of Australia, 2001).

A rights-based development strategy views participation from a rights-holder and duty-bearer perspective—on the one hand the aim is to enhance right's holders' capabilities to advocate for their entitlements so that they can define for themselves their own entry points for change. On the other hand, the strategy must address the duty-bearers' capacity to recognise, respect and fulfil the right to participation. It should deliberate the question: How can existing procedures, structures and processes be reformed or supplemented to secure free, active and meaningful participation of rights-holders?

As is seen from the above, participation and inclusion form a vital principle for the rights based approach. How does the practice of community work then reflect a rights-based approach? As mentioned earlier, the difference between rights based approach and the earlier approach is in the whole conceptualization of issues as 'problems or unmet needs' in the older approaches as compared to 'violations of rights or entitlements' in the rights based approach. The practice of community work then assumes a new dimension and conceptualization of issues as violations of rights or entitlements, demands a complementary 'duty bearer' entrusted with the responsibility of promoting, protecting such rights. A democratic and human-rights approach translates poor people's needs into rights, and recognises individuals as active subjects and stakeholders. It further identifies the obligations of states that are required to take steps—for example through legislation, policies and programmes—whose purpose is to respect, promote and fulfil the human rights of all people within their jurisdiction.

As Celestine N.M. & Andrea, C (2004) point out, 'most, if not all, (development) organisations see a 'rights-based' or 'human rights' approach as a catalyst that can transform the practice of development from a focus on identifying and meeting needs to enabling people to recognise and claim rights that are enshrined in the UDHR. For most, too, this entails (i) work with duty-holders—generally state, but also increasingly non-state actors—to strengthen their capacity to respond and be accountable in protecting, respecting and fulfilling human rights: what is termed as obligation, and accountability; and (ii) work to build the capacity of citizens to claim their rights, by working alongside them as advocates and by seeking to provide opportunities for people to empower themselves. The common principles of rights-based development, then, might be seen to reside in shifting how development actors 'do business', offering them—in theory—the potential to change their ways from unreflective patronage to the self-aware exercise of agency in support of those who are discriminated against and marginalised.

The paradigm of development and strategies being followed have undergone a sea change. Today there is more of a managerialism in terms of programmes and projects, yet there is scope for the process of participation and community work even within the tools developed by the managers of projects and programmes. Most international development and funding agencies insist on a sociological understanding of the communities their work is going to impact upon, participatory development of projects, stakeholders analysis and participatory concurrent monitoring of the projects. Within the whole cycle of projects and programmes there is an inbuilt component of people's participation. Moreover, the rights based approach is being followed in a large majority of such projects, be they concern environmental issues, watershed development, water-supply, health, forestry, micro finance, self help etc. Issues are being reformulated and positioned in a rights based perspective—the rights of indigenous people over minor forest produce, the rights of people to have access to natural resources, sustainable livelihoods, health, information etc.

The core concept of a right is that of an agreement or 'social contract' which is established between the person(s) who holds a right (often referred to as the 'rights-holder'), and the person(s) or institution(s) which then have obligations and responsibilities in relation to the realisation of that right (often referred to as the 'duty-bearer'). The responsibility for making sure that rights are respected, protected and fulfilled lies primarily with the state, in the form of the national government. But it also has implications for all elements of society from the level of international institutions, through to individuals in the family and community.

States have four types of obligations: to respect people's rights, to protect people's rights, to facilitate people's rights and to provide people's rights. As the primary duty bearer they have the main responsibility for bringing about the realisation of rights and are accountable both to the international community and to all people living within their borders. One of the offshoots of this process is the participation of the people in governance itself. It has increasingly been realized that governance, meaning thereby transparency, accountability, predictability and participation in the citizen-state relationship is one of the important components of development. It is in this process of governance, that the larger participation of communities is also sought. In India, with the 73rd and the 74th amendments to the Constitution of India, the participation of the community in matters related to their development has been ensured. A large number of government initiatives make statutory provisions of involving the people, more particularly the marginalized and oppressed sections of the community, like the Scheduled Castes, Scheduled Tribes, women and minorities. In addition, most developmental projects, initiated by the NGOs and INGOs, have an inbuilt component of participation, either in the form of project formulation committees, involving people in social analysis, stakeholders analysis, implementation committees, community monitoring and evaluation systems, user groups, etc.

The concept of community work and its scope is therefore also undergoing change. There is very little evidence of community organizing for organizing sake. Most NGOs are engaged in either implementation of projects or in advocacy and networking work on focused issues. As a result, the strategy of community work has to be now built into the project/programme cycle. What exactly is a Project? Put in simple terms, a project is an activity for which money will be spent in expectations of returns and which logically lends itself to planning, financing and implementation as a unit. It is perceived as an investment activity in which financial resources are expended to create capital assets that produce benefits over an extended period of time. Projects are the principal vehicles for transforming programmes and plans into action. They have been referred to as 'the cutting edge of development'. However, with more than half a century of development efforts, throughout the world, poverty still remains a pervasive issue.

On the other hand, there is donor fatigue and political interests in achieving the development goals have diminished. Issues like governance and corruption have come to assume significance. Yet, projects continue to be the cutting edge of development and will remain so in the foreseeable future too. It is convenient to think of the life of a project in terms of a cycle, comprising several distinct stages. Therefore, a number of international development agencies like the World Bank, the GTZ, and the IFAD have developed their own concept and interpretation of what a project cycle would look like.

2

Participation and the Participatory Approach

The principle of participation is widely recognised as a right in itself under the Declaration on the Right to Development. The right to take part in the conduct of public affairs (*article 25, ICCPR*) means that every person and all peoples are entitled to participate in, contribute to, and enjoy civil, economic, social and political development. It also means that all people are entitled to participate in society to the maximum of their potential. This, in turn, means that steps have to be taken to facilitate participation. This could include the provision of a supportive environment to enable people to develop and express their full potential and creativity. A rights-based strategy, therefore, aims for free, active and meaningful participation of targeted communities. 'Free' means participation that is voluntary and not imposed. 'Active' requires that the participation process has a certain direction; and 'meaningful' participation entails that it is consequential for goals achieved.

Participation as a concept has found favour and recently there have been quite a few arguments given for 'participation'. Croft & Beresford (1994) have elaborated on a few of such arguments.

Most people want to be involved: The ability and interest of the people to get involved is often limited by their deprived circumstances. However, it is seen that people have an intrinsic desire to get involved. This is reflected in the growth of various disability, rights and advocacy organizations.

People have a right to be involved: Social work can clearly impact on human rights, civil and legal rights. Social work interventions extend to the most personal and intimate aspects of peoples' lives. These interventions often have the power to restrict people's rights and have on occasions failed to respect them too. People have the legal entitlements to be involved, the rights to redress, to comment and to be consulted about social work and its interventions. If social work is to be a democratic activity, then the service users and other stakeholders have to be involved.

Involvement increases accountability: Accountability means not just being responsive but also answerable to the people. People have the right to know what is happening and why? Increased direct involvement of the service users results in more effective accountability of the service providers, often the state and NGOs.

Participation makes more efficient and cost-effective services: There is little clear evidence of a direct link between increased user involvement and enhanced efficiency and economy, yet, if social workers want to provide the support and services that people actually need, then involving them in the process is likely to avoid duplication and inappropriate provision, improve targeting and create pressure for more effective and responsive systems of management.

Involving people accords with Social Work goals: Peoples involvement is important because it is consistent with the aims of social work. Ideas of enabling and supporting people's independence and self determination cannot be achieved in an unequal relationship in which the 'client' has only a limited say and qualified involvement, which is located in an organisational setting over which he has no control. This creates more passivity and dependence and goes against the spirit of social work.

Involving people challenges institutionalized discrimination: Support services are often inaccessible to or inappropriate for marginalized, discriminated sections of the population. Involving service users and other people with all their diversity of age, race, class, gender, disability, sexual orientation etc.in all aspects of the intervention would directly challenge discrimination.

The main aim of social work practice is to empower people, so that they are able to challenge oppression and discrimination rather than reflecting them and making it possible for people to take greater charge of their lives. It allows people to participate in decisions concerning their lives instead of being in a receiving passive relationship with the agency. Such participation helps them to gain confidence, self esteem, assertiveness, expectations, knowledge and skills needed to have an effective say.

During the 1950s and 1960s, modernisation theories had been so pervasive that it was almost impossible to separate modernization from development linked to capitalism and economic growth. Economic development, i.e., increasing productivity of labour and raising standards of living was perceived as critical to modernization. Criticism of the trickle-down theory and the growing realization that mainstream development strategies were losing the battle against poverty and hunger, prompted a shift away from the modernization approach to modernization with a human face—the basic needs approach. The basic needs approach advocated a shift from the high technology, top-down development strategy to provide the minimum standard of living which a society should set for the poorest of its people.

Gunnar Myrdal, the Nobel Prize winning Swedish economist, in the late 1960s urged governments to plan their economies actively, adopt social policies that enhanced people's welfare and take steps to redistribute income and wealth. This led to the publication of a major policy document from the United Nations (1971), 'Social Policy and Planning in National Development', that contained practical recommendations on the establishment of social planning units in the central planning ministries to formulate social sector plans. Social planning began to emerge as the best means to promote unified socio-economic development and the most popular social development strategy formulated in the 1970s, the basic needs approach, began to take shape. As a strategy, basic needs 'seeks to mobilize resources for social development. By putting priority on education, village health services, literacy and similar social programmes, it addresses the root problems of underdevelopment' (Midgley, 1995). As development was being understood at the household and individual level, it was realized that women were central to the provision of basic needs as they carried out the important roles of food production, family consumption and birth control in the family. The basic needs strategy thus made possible the inclusion of social justice issues, such as gender equality and indigenous rights, in development agenda from 1970s onwards (See Schech S. & Haggis J, 2000).

However, as Midgely (1995) points out, the approaches (basic needs along with unified socio-economic planning and redistribution with growth) assumed that the governments would promote social development efficiently and justly. Some proponents of social development believed instead that social development could best be fostered through the efforts of ordinary people themselves. This led to the formulation of the popular participation approach. As Midgley *et al.* (1986) have noted the notion of popular participation and that of community participation were interlinked. The former was concerned with broad issues of social development and the creation of opportunities for the involvement of people in the political, economic and social life of a nation, the latter connotes the direct involvement of ordinary people in local affairs.

People centered development puts people as the major propeller and major recipients of development. It is people first; people working for other people; and people actualizing themselves as fulfilled human beings. If people centered development is pursued, the focal point is communities and not industries or sectors. As a corollary, three concepts emerge. First, development is a community or societal effort. Second, development is collaboration, the joint harnessing and utilization of resources by people adopting mutually beneficial strategies. Third, development is not for the privileged few but for all. Central to the concept of people centered development is empowerment of the people. People must get involved and participate fully in the social, economic, political, cultural and spiritual aspects of their development. They must have access to resources, whether financial, natural, physical or human in order to participate. Finally, they must have the capacity to manage themselves, their organisations and their resources. People must build their own capabilities to provide for their basic needs and more.

It is noteworthy however, that the concept of participatory development had been experimented with in India, much before it took shape in the development discourse. The Community Development Programme, launched in 1952 initially in 55 Community Development Blocks of the country was characterized as a programme of 'aided self help', and intended to be planned and implemented by the villagers themselves, government offering technical and financial assistance. V.T. Krishnamachari, Deputy Chairman of the Planning Commission at that time and a doyen of the Community Development Programme had cautioned that 'we should give up the idea that we are here to force our programme and plans on the villagers. It is for the villagers to tell us what they want and for us to assist them (quoted in Jain, L.C., *et al.,* 1985). It is unfortunate however, that the Government of India, in the light of various negative assessments, chose to abandon the programme as well as its participatory approach after some time. One of the legacies of the period, the Panchayati Raj Institution of decentralized planning and administration, have however been revitalized recently through the 73rd and 74th Amendments to the Constitution of India.

As mentioned earlier, the trickle-down theory based on the top down approach to social and economic planning did not yield the anticipated results. Whatever results were obtained through this approach also did not appear sustainable. Bureaucrats, technocrats, administrators and development agents (extension workers) showed an utter lack of zeal, transparency and accountability in administering the development programmes. The development administration became self-serving and self perpetuating, ignoring the perspective, aspirations, needs, problems and resources of the common masses. Responsiveness and ownership from the people was also found lacking.

In addition, around 1960s, it was realized the world over, that the findings of conventional and laboratory based agricultural research were irrelevant and not based on real life situations of the farmers. Scientific research appeared to devalue the centuries old indigenous knowledge of the farmers and sometimes almost obliterated it. There was thus a 'need to find a research method that would give powers to the powerless and make people the subject and not the object of research'. In addition, 'there was also an intellectual ferment that permeated the academe during the 1960s that questioned the ivory tower stance of research and how the results were being used' (See IFAD, ANGOC and IIRR, 2001).

One of the major influences on the development of the participatory approach worldwide has been the seminal and decisive work by Paulo Freire. In his 'Pedagogy of the Oppressed', Freire (1970) put forward his basic premise that the poor and the marginalized are capable of analysing their own realities, reflect upon them and consequently bring about change in their situation. He urged for the creation of conditions under which the poor and the marginalized would be enabled to develop 'critical consciousness' or 'conscientisation'. This conscientisation model was experimented with in the adult education movement and acted as an impetus for the development of participatory methods. Freire's quest was to identify a process of critical discovery through which oppressed people could free their minds and become aware that they hold the key to transformative change. He identified the way in which perceptions of powerlessness erode hope and create a culture of silence. Concientisation is a process by which people become aware of the political, socio-economic and cultural contradictions that interact in a hegemonic way to diminish their lives. Conscientisation, process of becoming critically aware, to Friere had three levels, magical consciousness, naïve consciousness and critical consciousness. Magical consciousness refers to the levels at which people are passive and unquestioning about the injustices in their lives. Things are passively accepted and explanations are often based on fatalism, such as the explanation of their present predicaments and sufferings to their deeds of the past or sins. In naïve consciousness, there is a degree of insight into the nature of individual problems, but it does not connect to structural discrimination. People normally blame themselves for their sufferings like that they should have studied harder while at school etc. This individualization of problems lends itself to the hegemonic blaming of victims. Critical consciousness is the stage at which connections are made with the way in which structures of the society discriminate, reaching into people's being, shaping their lives in prejudiced ways. The process is rooted in critical reflection and collective struggle (Ledwith M., 1997).

Analyses and examinations of underdevelopment in the late 1970s and 1980s brought up explanations of the causes of people's poverty and suggested different forms of project design. As a result of these analyses, the poor people were viewed as excluded and marginalised both from broader societal participation and also from direct involvement in development initiatives. Simultaneously, development policy makers and planners began to argue for societal level political participation and also to devise strategies whereby poor people could become more directly involved in development efforts.

In development terms efforts to promote people's participation in development, which would involve a fundamental shift—both in attitudes and in methodology—if it was to break decades of top-down, non-participatory practice were initiated. Since the early 1990s, the major donor development agencies recognising the problems caused by non-participatory development have put their weight behind and committed resources to promoting participatory development.

Participation has been understood at various levels by different authors and agencies. Conceptualisations of participation have ranged from 'contributions by the people to public programmes' to the 'involvement of people in the entire decision making process'. The very minimalist definition of participation has been provided by the Economic Commission of Latin America (*ECLA*) in 1973. According to the ECLA 'Participation is defined as a voluntary contribution by the people in one or another of the public programmes supposed to contribute to national development, but the people are not expected to take part in shaping the programme or in criticizing its contents'. A much more comprehensive definition has been provided by Cohen and Uphoff (1980) whose conceptualization of participation 'includes peoples involvement in decision making processes, in implementing programmes, their sharing in benefits of development programmes and their involvement in efforts to evaluate such programmes'.

In the late 1960s there was a series of debates around 'participation' (see, for example, Pateman 1970). While 'participation' may be a vague term, its advocates often rely on two key arguments about its value. It:

- makes for justice in decision-making—people have some say in, and influence on, collective decisions.
- has an educative value. Through participation people learn (Beetham, 1992).

These interests became formalized in a number of United Nations reports including Popular Participation in Development (1971) and Popular Participation in Decision Making for Development (1975).

The United Nations document on Popular Participation as a Strategy for Planning Community Level Action and National Development (1981), defined community participation as 'the creation of opportunities to enable all members of a community to actively contribute to and influence the development process and to share equitably in the fruits of development'.

Beginning late 1970s, there have been various interpretations of the concept of participation. Cohen and Uphoff's interpretation of participation has already been described earlier. Paul (1987) defines it 'an active process by which beneficiary or client groups influence the direction and execution of a development project with a view of enhancing their well-being in terms of income, personal growth, self-reliance or other values they cherish' Participatory development has been looked at as a partnership which is built upon the basis of dialogue among the various actors, during which the agenda is jointly set, and local views and indigenous knowledge are deliberately sought and respected. This implies negotiation rather than the dominance of an externally set project agenda. Thus people become actors instead of being beneficiaries.

Participation is also seen as a process whereby local people cooperate or collaborate with externally introduced development programmes or projects. In this way participation becomes the means whereby such initiatives can be more effectively implemented. People's participation is sponsored by an external agency and it is seen as a technique to support the progress of the programme or project. The term 'participatory development' is more commonly used to describe this approach and it implies externally designed development activities implemented in a participatory manner. This approach appears to be quite widespread and essentially promotes participation as a means of ensuring the successful outcome of the activities undertaken.

Participation is often seen as a goal in itself. This goal can be expressed as the empowering of people in terms of their acquiring the skills, knowledge and experience to take greater responsibility for their development. People's poverty can often be explained in terms of their exclusion and lack of access to and control of the resources that they need to sustain and improve their lives. Participation is an instrument of change that can help to break that exclusion and provide poor people with the basis for their more direct involvement in development initiatives.

As the typology given by Oakley (1991) demonstrates, participation has been considered as contribution, organization and empowering. As contribution, participation includes voluntary or other contribution made by people to various programmes and projects in return for some perceived benefits. Few researchers view organization as a fundamental instrument of participation, either as externally conceived or emerging as a result of the process of participation. Participation is considered as empowering when some kind of power is achieved, people have access to and control of resources, and work towards structural change.

The FAO typology looks at participation from three perspectives: functional, empowering and philosophical. Functional participation means participation to increase the efficiency and effectiveness of research and development. Empowering participation is meant to increase the independence, awareness and capacity of marginalized groups, while philosophical participation allows the expression of alternate views.

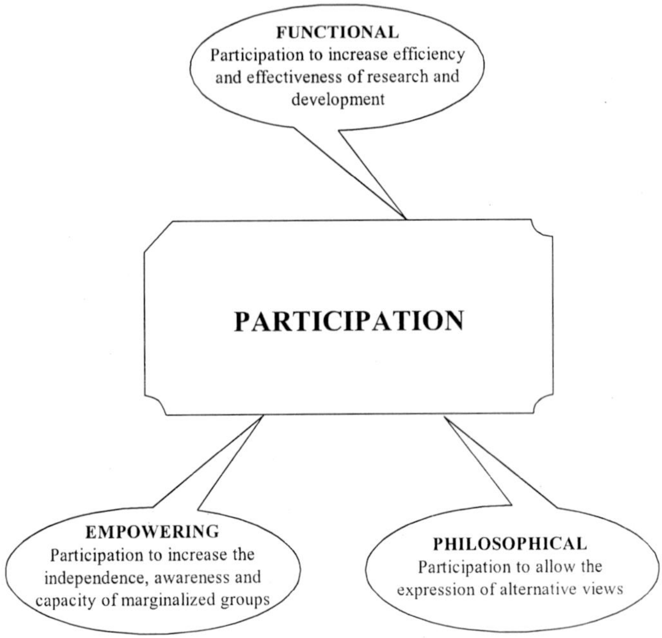

Source: http://www.fao.org/Participation/english_web_new/content_en/project_part.html

As Rahnema in the Development Dictionary, (1992) narrates, participation could be transitive or intransitive; moral, amoral or immoral; either forced or free; either manipulative or spontaneous. Transitive participation is oriented towards a goal (project or political context), whereas an intransitive participation is one that is without pre-designed purposes. This includes recovery of ones own inner freedom, of loving, of creating, and other similar processes. This aspect of participation has been largely ignored in development discourse and deserves attention. Manipulative participation is one where it is driven by the agenda of the donor, government or the NGO sector. Often governments manipulate participation to gain greater productivity at lower cost by making the poor bear the cost. It is also often used to negotiate and reduce resistance to conventional development policy and programmes. It is also important to recognise that some activists and NGOs also 'suffer from existential duality of the oppressed', thus manipulate participation for maintaining their control over the community. Manipulators need not always be outsiders, often community leaders and members, enter into participation, by manipulating other community members and often by coopting members into the programme.

Jules N. has also drawn a typology of participation in development programmes. For him participation extends from manipulative to self-mobilisation. Manipulative participation is pretence with non-elected people's representatives, they have no power. When people are informed of predecided events and activities and their response is ignored, it is classified as passive participation. Often people are consulted, problems are defined by external agents, who also control the information gathering and analysis; people thus do not participate in the decision making. Such participation has been termed as participation by consultation. Sometimes participation is for material incentives; when people participate by contributing resources (labour) for material incentives, but are not involved in the learning process. Functional participation is when the external agency sees it as a means to achieve project goals or predetermined objectives. However there is shared decision making but only on minor activities. Interactive participation is when people are involved in joint analysis, action plan development, and formation and strengthening of local institutions. People have control over local and resource use decisions. Self mobilization occurs when independent initiatives are taken by the people to change systems; they contact external agencies for resource and technical advice, control resource use and may or may not challenge existing distribution of power and wealth.

Participation is also operationalised at several levels. Ranging from material contribution to empowerment, participation varies in the nature of community involvement. IIED (1996) has outlined an eight-stage typology of participation. At the most basic level is the passive participation where people participate by being told what is going to happen or has already happened and the highest level is that of catalyzing change, where the community members have a stake and are involved in influencing others in the environment to initiate change:

(a) *Passive participation*: People participate by being told what is going to happen or has already happened. A unilateral announcement is made by the administration or project management without listening to people's responses. The information being shared belongs to external professionals.

(b) *Participation in information giving*: People participate by answering questions posed by extractive researchers using questionnaire surveys or similar approaches. People do not have the opportunity to influence proceedings, as the findings of the research are neither shared nor checked for accuracy.

(c) *Participation by consultation*: People participate by being consulted, and external people listen to views. These external professionals define both problems and solutions, and may modify these in the light of people's responses. Such a consultative process does not concede any share in decision making, and professionals are under no obligation to take on board people's views.

(d) *Participation for material incentives*: People participate by providing resources such as labour, in return for food, cash or other material incentives. Most on-farm research today falls in this category-farmers provide the fields for demonstration but are not involved in the experimentation or the process of learning. It is very common to see this called participation, yet people have no stake in prolonging activities when the incentives end.

(e) *Functional participation*: People participate by forming groups, which are externally initiated to meet predetermined objectives related to the project. Involvements of the community is not solicited at early stages of the project cycle but rather after major decisions have been made. These groups tend to be dependent on external initiators and facilitators, but may eventually become self dependent.

(f) *Interactive participation*: People participate in joint analysis, which leads to action plans and the formation of new local institutions or the strengthening of existing ones. These groups take control over local decisions, and so people have a stake in maintaining structures or practices.

(g) *Self-mobilisation*: People participate by taking initiatives to change systems independent of external institutions. They develop contacts with external institutions for resources and technical advice they need, but retain control over how resources are used. Such self-initiated mobilization and collective action may or may not challenge existing inequitable distributions of wealth and power.

(h) *Catalysing change*: An eighth level of participation may be added to this typology, viz, the involvement and stakes of community members in influencing others in the environment to initiate change.

Another typology on participation has been provided by the FAO. As the FAO manual on participation lists it, people can participate in various ways, from information receiving to empowerment (www.fao.org).

Participation by Information: Receiving underpins all other levels of participation, and may be appropriate on its own in some circumstances. People participate by being told what is going to happen or has already happened. It is unilateral announcement by an administration or programme management without listening to people's responses. The information being shared belongs only to external professionals.

Participation in Information Giving: Lets people participate by answering questions posed by extractive researchers and programme managers using questionnaire surveys or similar approaches. People do not have the opportunity to influence proceedings, as the findings of the research or programme design are neither shared nor checked for accuracy.

Consultation: People participate by being consulted, and external agents listen to views. These external agents define both problems and solutions, and may modify these in the light of people's responses. Such a consultative process does not concede any share in decision-making and professionals are under no obligation to take on board peoples' views.

Joint Planning: People participate in joint analysis, which leads to action plans and the formulation of new local groups or strengthening of existing ones. It tends to involve interdisciplinary methodologies that seek multiple perspectives and make use of systematic and structured learning processes. These groups take control over local decisions, so people have a stake in maintaining structures and practices.

Decision Making: When consensus is acted upon through collective decisions, this marks the initiation of shared responsibilities for outcomes that may result. Negotiations at this stage reflect different degrees of leverage exercised by individuals and groups.

Empowerment: People participate in joint analysis, which leads to action plans and the formulation of new local groups or strengthening of existing ones. These groups take control over local decisions, so people have a stake in maintaining structures and practices. People participate by taking initiatives independent of external institutions to change systems. Such self-initiated mobilisation and collective action may or may not challenge inequitable distributions of wealth or power.

As Mickkelsen (1995) points out, 'the two major uses of participation centre around participation as an end in itself or as a means to development'. These are not two ends of a continuum; rather they represent transformational participation and instrumental participation and often appear in different combinations in a project. As an end, participation leads to empowerment; that is, the local community has the right and capability to have a say in decisions concerning their lives. Participation thus becomes an 'instrument in the promotion of ideological or normative goals such as social justice, equity and democracy'. On the other hand, participation is viewed as a means to ensuring efficiency in project management; it becomes a tool in the implementation of developmental interventions.

Two Logical models Underlying Participatory Strategies

Strategy	*Efficiency*	*Empowerment*
	State building through top down partnership with local population/civil society/the poor (inclusive reaching down)	Alternative development defined by local popular movements and organiza-tions(integrative reaching up)
Normative assumptions	The poor masses ought to have satisfied their basic needs (as they are defined by the state)	The poor masses ought to get the kind of development decided by themselves
Deductive assumptions	This presupposes their participation in the public development programmes. Therefore they must be made capable of participating more	This presupposes an actively formulating and organizing population having the ability and the rights to express their demands
Causal theoretical assumptions	Development goals can be reached harmoniously and conflicts between social groups resolved through some kind of local democracy. Therefore people's participation is possible	Development goals can be reached harmoniously and conflicts between social groups resolved through some kind of local democracy. Therefore people's participation is possible
	People's participation has a positive effect on development	Development is positive when there is people's participation
	People's participation is an effective means to mobilize local (human and material) resources with the purpose of implementing (certain) development programmes	Empowerment of the masses is a necessary means to achieve people's participation, as no government will spend any resources on development and welfare decided by the masses unless these masses have the power to force the government

(contd.)

(contd.)

Strategy	*Efficiency*	*Empowerment*
	Lack of participation is an expression of the population's inability to participate: lack of education, lack of funds and resources, low level of organisation	Lack of popular participation in development programmes is an expression of disagreement or resistance (internally amongst members of the local community or externally against the central government or the people in power)
	Or it is an expression of the programme design being inappropriately adapted to the needs of the target group, *i.e.* inappropriate planning and implementing procedures, or inappropriate technology. (operational barriers to participation)	Or it is an expression of the existence of social structures excluding the masses from participating.
	Thus it is a technical, educational, administrative, or financial inadequacy needing to be corrected.	Thus it is a social conflict to be resolved through a compromise on conflicting policies and/or removal of the 'departicipatory' social structures.

Source: Mikkelsen (1995)

De-centralisation and Participation: A key element in empowering local communities to take decisions is the process of decentralization. Decentralisation implies increased authority, responsibility and resources to local bodies to plan, manage and coordinate development activities by themselves. India experimented with decentralized development with the advent of the Community Development Programme in early 1950s. Panchayati Raj Institutions (PRI) and Urban Local Bodies were entrusted with the responsibility of their own development. The experiment did not succeed for long and except for a few states, the panchayati raj institutions withered. It is recently with the passing of the 73rd and 74th amendments to the Constitution of India, that the Panchayati Raj Institutions and Urban Local Bodies have been revived and given extensive powers including the power to raise revenue. An interesting step within the amendments is the reservation of close to one-third of the seats to the PRIs for women. Mixed reports have emanated from the field on this initiative, some encouraging, some not very encouraging. However the need for enabling participation and capacity building has emerged very strongly. Two important areas require urgent attention, one, to ensure participation and to sustain the process at an institutional level by social mobilisation and second, the need for human resource development to strengthen the Panchayati Raj Institutions as self-governing institutions.

The critical issue to bear in mind is that people's participation in development is concerned with two things: (i) structural relationships and the importance of developing people's capacities and skills to negotiate and to seek the resources and changes which they require in order to improve their lives; and (ii) the methods and techniques whereby local people can be brought to play a part and to develop a stake in development programmes and projects. Both purposes are of equal importance; the former seeks to secure a longer term and sustainable development for poor people, the latter is crucial in providing immediate access to the benefits of development.

Participation and Project Cycle Management: One of the ways in which developmental activity takes place is through projects. A project is a scheme to organize the use of a given quantity of resources in a specific way to achieve particular results, all within a definite time. It has a precise beginning and a precise end. The execution of a project requires multidisciplinary effort, mobilizing different skills and resources to achieve predetermined development objectives, which will result, directly or indirectly, in new or added value or social, economic or financial benefits.

Within this general definition many different examples of projects can be described, each with a different type of organization. However, they all have the same fundamental parts or phases, from the time each project is first conceptualized until it is terminated. These parts fit together and relate to each other in what is called the project cycle. The cycle represents a continuous process in which each stage provides the foundation for the next.

Many international development organizations and institutions divide the project cycle in roughly five stages in the cycle of existence of a project, namely, identification, preparation, appraisal and agreement, implementation, and monitoring and evaluation.

At project identification the project idea is translated into a preliminary description of the project. Terms of reference for the project reconnaissance team are established, analyses of existing situations are performed, a broad evaluation of the future "with" and "without" the project is made, and the extent and limits of the project are proposed. Different approaches to the project are identified, and a judgment made regarding which option should be taken forward to project preparation.

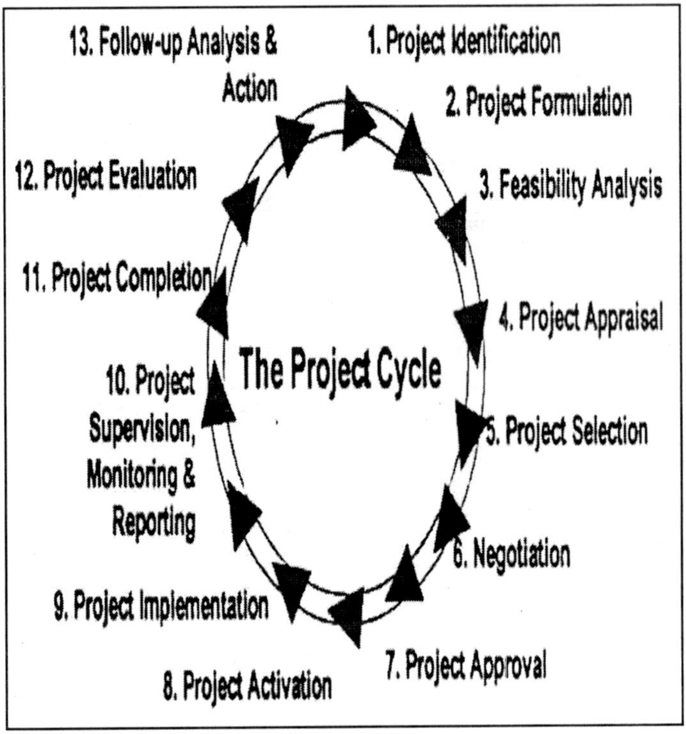

FIGURE : PROJECT CYCLE

At project preparation stage, the project is designed. Objectives, pre-requisites, inputs, outputs, organization, participants, clearances are all defined, costs and earnings are calculated, a financial plan is prepared, expected results are analysed, the socio-economic and environmental impacts are estimated, and the provisional and final project documents are prepared.

At project appraisal and agreement stage, appraisal documents are prepared from the project documents and a succession of appraisal meetings, clearances, and financing negotiations take place. This brings the project to the point of meeting the required start-up agreement conditions, sometimes after revision and adaptation of project schedule, cost, objectives, and financing.

In project implementation phase, the project management and lines of command are established, and various implementation procedures established. In the course of implementation, project progress is monitored, revisions and adaptations are made for unexpected events, and finally the project is brought to completion.

At project evaluation stage, which takes place at a suitable time after the project has been implemented, project objectives, project implementation, and project benefits are appraised. This evaluation may result in the project being extended or in the identification of a new project, and may lead to a revision of the method(s) by which similar projects will be formulated in the future.

Projects vary in scale, purpose and duration. They may be initiated within a community, requiring modest inputs and producing tangible outputs within a relatively short timeframe. At the other extreme, projects may require substantial financial resources and only generate benefits in the long term. For example, the former could be an adult literacy project in a village; the latter may be the provision of universal primary education for all children of school age in a country. Whilst the former needs one trainer and a few teaching materials, the latter requires numerous schools, teachers, equipment and administration. Projects may stand-alone or be integrated into a programme, with several projects contributing to one overall goal.

With the project approach, the key priority issue for participatory projects is how to ensure the participation of project beneficiaries in all stages of the project cycle. For example, in the case of community forestry projects, what methods can be used to ensure that the forest users are actively involved in forest-management? Or in the case of rural water supply projects, how can water users effectively participate in the design, implementation and long term management of water systems.

Groups and Community Work: Much of community work takes place through the medium of groups. Presently in a project mode groups are being used on an extensive scale, they could be self help groups, user groups, monitoring groups, or simple community groups to effectively participate in all aspects of a project. It is important to have a look at what groups are and how do these groups stay together—something of prime importance in participatory community work.

The scientific study of groups began at the turn of the century. A question, which continues to receive much attention, concerns the extent to which being a part of a group influences the group member. Early findings suggested that the presence of others has a significant influence on an individual group member. The presence of others tends to generate pressure to conform to the standards of behaviour that are expected of those who belong to the group.

Bon L (1910), referred to the forces that were generated by group interaction as 'group contagion' and 'group mind', recognizing that people in groups react differently than individuals. Kurt Lewin in his famous 'field theory' brings out that "a group has a life space". It occupies a position relative to other objects in space, it is oriented towards goals, it locomotes in pursuit of these goals and it may encounter barriers in the process of locomotion (Shepard C, 1964).

Field theory views the group as a gestalt, i.e. an entity of opposing forces that act to hold members in the group and to move the group along in its quest for goal achievement. Groups are constantly changing to cope with their social situation, although there are times when a 'quasi-stationery equilibrium' exists for all groups. In all cases, however, the behaviour of individual group members and the group itself must be seen as a function of the total situation (Lewin K, 1947).

Social Exchange theorists suggest that when people interact in groups, each will attempt to behave in a way that will maximize rewards and minimize punishments. Group members initiate interactions because these social exchanges provide them with something of value, such as approval. On the other hand, to system theorists like Parsons (1951), groups are social systems with several interdependent members attempting to maintain order and a stable equilibrium while they function as a unified whole. Groups are constantly facing changing demands in their quest to attain goals and to maintain a stable equilibrium. They must mobilize their resources and act to meet changing demands if they are to survive. According to Parsons, groups must accomplish the following four functional tasks to remain in equilibrium:

(a) Integration-ensuring that members of groups fit together;
(b) Adaptation-ensuring that groups change to cope with demands of the environment;
(c) Pattern maintenance-ensuring that groups define and sustain their basic purposes, identities, and procedures; and
(d) Goal attainment-ensuring that groups pursue and accomplish their tasks.

The likelihood that a group will survive also depends on the demands of the environment, the extent to which members identify with group goals, and the degree to which members believe goals are attainable. By overcoming obstacles and successfully handling the functional tasks confronting them, groups strive to remain in a state of equilibrium.

Cohesion, the totality of forces acting on individual members to keep them in the group, has been shown to be related to agreement on goals and norms, shared understanding and similar demographic backgrounds of members as well as to productivity, satisfaction, and cooperative interaction patterns. As pointed out by Cartwright (1968), four interacting sets of variables determine a member's attraction to a group:

(a) the need for affiliation, recognition, and security;
(b) incentives and resources available through the group such as prestige of the members, the group goals, its program activities, and its style of operation;
(c) the subjective expectations of members about the beneficial or detrimental consequences of the group; and
(d) a comparison of the group to other group experiences.

Mckean, Margaret A. (1987) highlights salient features of successful groups:

(i) Community of owners have to be well defined, self-conscious and self-governing with political independence to act collectively, as it deems appropriate;
(ii) The distribution of rights in and benefits to collective good has to be a careful balance of the inegalitarian and egalitarian traits that is economically efficient;
(iii) Rules must be easily enforced, highly specific and conservative with regard to the sustainability of collective action; and
(iv) Enforcement of rules must be member themselves rather than by an overlord of super-ordinate authority of government to ensure that, it is both thorough and impartial.

Buchanan and Tullock (1965) have elaborated on the conditions under which a group would choose a collective mode of action. They point out that it is possible when each of its individual members finds it profitable to act collectively rather than individually, *i.e.* when his perceived costs are less than his perceived benefits from the collective action. The perceived costs include both external costs and decision making costs. Similarly, Olson (1965) says that in smaller groups, each of the members or majority of the members find that his private gain from the collective good or activity is more than his private gain from doing it individually.

Hardin (1968) points out that collective action fails when the perceived private costs to the individuals of cooperating exceed the perceived private benefits of cooperating. Mckean (1987) has also elaborated on two more reasons for the failure of collective action:

(i) When individuals feel that their own contribution to the collective good is miniscule and would not be missed if withheld because others will continue contributing, enabling them easily to free ride on the contribution of others; and

(ii) When individuals have no assurance or certainty that other members of the group will make their contributions or cooperate; and their lone contribution to the effort would be sufficient to produce the desired outcome.

Groups, being dynamic, evolve and develop over time. Many attempts have been made to classify stages of group development and various models of group development have appeared in literature. As Toseland and Rivas (1995) point out, little evidence exists to support the notion that any one model accurately describes the stages through which all groups pass. Overall, the studies that have been conducted suggest that groups move through stages, but that the stages are not constant across different groups.

Participatory Rural Appraisal: One of the earliest pioneers in participatory work was Robert Chambers, who developed a technique known as the Rapid Rural Appraisal (RRA). RRA attempted to incorporate the interests of the poor and marginalized in development interventions. It acknowledged the need to consult the poor on their needs. RRA however was seen as a means of information gathering by the outsiders and was therefore replaced by PRA or the Participatory Rural Appraisal that empowered the local masses. Through PRA communities look at their situation in-depth, measure their capacities and capabilities, frame issues and interventions and initiate the process of change with themselves being the main actors. Communities are facilitated to articulate their issues and concerns through the means of various methods of PRA. A number of other approaches like Participatory Learning and Action (PLA), Rapid Participatory Rural Appraisal (RPRA), Visualisation in Participatory Programme (VIPP) are also currently being used; however, they all essentially build upon the RRA/PRA.

PRA can be described as a family of approaches, methods and behaviours that enable people to express and analyse the realities of their lives and conditions, to plan themselves what action to take, and to monitor and evaluate the results. Its methods have evolved from Rapid Rural Appraisal (RRA). The difference is that PRA emphasises processes that empower local people, whereas RRA is mainly seen as a means for outsiders to gather information. The terminology is confusing and there is much debate about what constitutes "real" PRA. The key elements of PRA are the methods used, and—most importantly—the behaviour and attitudes of those who facilitate it (IDS 1996). PRA has much in common with RRA but differs basically in the ownership of information and the nature of the process: in RRA information is more elicited and extracted by outsiders as part of the process of data gathering; in PRA it is more generated, analysed, owned and shared by local people as part of the process of their empowerment (Chambers R, 1994a). Both RRA and PRA share a set of principles. As Chambers puts it, the principles of RRA and PRA have 'been induced rather than deduced, they have been elicited by trying out practices, finding what works and what does not, and then asking why'. Some of the common principles that are shared by both RRA and PRA include:

- A reversal of learning, to learn from local people directly, face to face and gain insight from their local physical, technical and social knowledge;
- Learning rapidly and progressively, with conscious exploration, flexible use of methods, opportunism, improvisation, iteration, and cross checking, not following a blue print programme but being adaptable in a learning process;

- Offsetting biases, especially those of rural development tourism, by being relaxed and not rushing, listening not lecturing, probing instead of passing on to the next topic, being unimposing instead of important, and seeking out the poorer people and women and learning from their concerns and priorities;
- Optimising trade-offs, relating the costs of learning to the useful truth of information, with trade-offs between quantity, relevance, accuracy and timeliness. This includes the principle of optimal ignorance-knowing what it is not worth knowing, and of appropriate imprecision-not measuring more than needed;
- Triangulating, meaning using a range of methods, types of information, investigators, and/or disciplines to cross check;
- Seeking diversity, that is seeking variability rather than averages. It goes beyond the crosschecking of triangulation; for defined broadly, it deliberately looks for, notices and investigates contradictions, anomalies and differentness (Chambers R, 1992).

The paradigm of development has been undergoing a major shift in recent times. As mentioned earlier, the limitations of the top-down approach have led to the propagation of the bottoms-up approach. The theoretical approaches are becoming more practical and field based. Development agencies and functionaries are more interested in participatory processes rather than chasing 'targets' and people are increasingly being looked as 'participants' or 'stakeholders in' rather than 'objects of' development.

'The clear message of the new paradigm is learning from the field, learning to respect and recognise field knowledge and experience, listening to alternative perspectives, appreciating other peoples reality and learning through hands-on practice' (Mukherjee N, 2002). Mukherjee has outlined five important issues concerning the paradigmatic shift:

- Whose reality counts?

- Whose world-view is neglected?
- What is this development all about?
- Development-Who owns it? and
- Social exclusion and power relations;

There is now increasing recognition that people have their own reservoir of knowledge, popularly known as indigenous traditional knowledge (ITK). Earlier approaches did not appreciate the ITK or the potential of the people to understand their own reality and thereby secure sustainable solutions to their problems. Solutions conjured up by technocrats without paying heed to indigenous knowledge has been risky and achieved little success. Increasingly development agencies are engaged in documenting the oral tradition and knowledge of communities to understand the 'reality'. Neela Mukherjee points out that ITK is important because such knowledge is contextual, includes answers to many questions, augments problem solving abilities of both local communities and external agencies and helps in probing relational linkages between issues and causal factors from different dimensions.

One of the factors is the recognition that there are multiple perspectives of the local communities, who have different world views. If determination of the priorities and preferences of the local communities is to be in the right direction, there has to be increasing appreciation of the multiple perspectives and world views. What is important is that there is not only appreciation of the multiple perspectives and world view but also creation of legitimate space for their involvement and enhancing their problem-solving abilities for the future.

The conventional objective of development has been to meet targets of the projects. The human factor seems to be missing in the race to achieve targets. As Mukherjee (2002) points out, however, 'in the changing paradigm human development is emerging as the ultimate objective in terms of gaining sustainable livelihood, actualization of human needs and community empowerment in the larger context'.

The ultimate test for any developmental project is the sustainability of its momentum after the project life is over. This has direct connection with the ownership of the project by the local communities and their involvement in all aspects of the project. Often the goods and services provided under the project do not prove to be durable and continuous. Also, the quality of such deliverables is often questionable. Beneficiaries also may not be satisfied with the deliverable since they do not meet their needs and priorities but those perceived as important by the agency. In addition, the services etc., may not be accessible to all, particularly the marginalized and dispossessed. In the absence of local involvement in all stages of the project, their capacity to handle the post-project activities (after the project is over) is also severely hampered. Overlooking the human aspects of the project at the cost of physical targets is a serious lacuna in the traditional development initiatives. This brings out the need for building strong institutions at the grass-roots.

There is increasing recognition among the discriminated and marginalized that the conventional development models have favoured the rich and the powerful. As a result, such groups have started questioning the models, but this is largely in areas where NGOs and other movements have helped in raising their consciousness regarding their rights. This is unfortunately not very widespread. There is however some recognition that the power relations need to be recalibrated and made more fair and equitable to the benefit of the marginalized.

Participatory methods are to be used not only for improving the quality of programme delivery, but also to transform the root causes of poverty and social exclusion. It is important to understand the role of participation and transformation in shifting the deeply entrenched forces of power and exclusion. There is need to examine the contribution of the language of rights and advocacy to this process. As Pettit & Musyoki (2004) acknowledge, many participatory efforts have not led to fundamental change, even where so intended and the two core principles of participation and transformation have often failed to converge. Often, the forces have proven to be resilient to change and participatory processes have often been overcome by 'the system and power relations they were expected to transform'.

Putting Rights, Participation and Power into Practice

Rights	*Participation*	*Power*
constructing collective identities	motivating protagonism in the community	participating in civil society networks and forums
campaigns (local, regional, national)	mobilizing new leaders	mobilizing new leaders
participating in civil society networks and forums	capacitation and formation (workshops, seminars, courses etc)	motivating protagonism in the community
pressure/lobby to create laws and public policies	capacitation in practice (meetings, actions, councils)	democratizing information
conducting alternative actions of public politics	community educator	participating in councils and other organs of social control
participating in councils	joint effort groups	participatory methodologies such as reflect-action
legal advisement	participatory management of the entity and projects	participatory methodologies of evaluation and projects
democratizing information about already existing rights	participatory methodologies of evaluation and projects	participatory management of the entity and projects
capacitation and formation (workshops, seminars, courses etc)	participation in civil society networks and forums	community educator
community educator	participating in councils and other organs of social control	capacitation and formation (workshops, seminars, courses etc)
income-generating projects	participating in participatory budgeting	income-generating projects
community radio	presenting their actions	rotating fund for community development

Source: Junior, Atune and Romano, 2004

From a human rights perspective, the framing of development goals as articulated in the Universal Declaration and other covenants, has helped in leveraging changes in favour of the poor and others whose dignity and rights were violated. Following a legal rights approach opens up opportunities for advocacy, education and legislative action that has the potential for transformation. Power sensitive participatory approach can 'allow people to develop their own awareness and knowledge as a basis for their empowered action to name and claim rights'.

It is important to recognise that methods are not sufficient in the absence of a clear vision and strategy. There is need for inclusive processes for developing long term visions of change, and to locate the use of tools and methods within strategies that are sensitive to the context of power. Rights and development should not be seen as distinct approaches, but as complementary and continuous approaches. As Pettit & Musyoki (2004) put it 'the denial of rights and exclusion of people from decision making and access to resources are usually reinforced by deeply embedded social and cultural relations of power. Changing such power relations is a long-term, many staged process, and often begins with processes of transformative learning with the less powerful in order to build awareness, legitimize alternate sources of knowledge and values, and strengthen self confidence'. One of the important aspects of rights based approach and advocacy work is the recognition of the state, both as a duty bearer as well as an important player in the development process. The rights based approach seeks to make the roles and responsibilities of the state more categorical and demonstrative, to raise public awareness of these commitments, and to demand responsiveness, accountability and transparency. Participatory approaches have been able to deepen and intensify the voices of the marginalized and engaging the state at different levels, through participatory advocacy, policy processes, and systems of democracy and governance.

3

Attitudes and Skills in Participatory Community Work

How does the rights language and discourse translate into practical rights based community work? What impact does the language of rights have on our approach towards development and people? How do we as social workers incorporate the spirit of rights in our day-to-day work? What roles are envisaged for a community worker under the rights based perspective? These are various questions that confront the community worker intending to take up rights based community work. In addition and more importantly, how do social work and social workers who have traditionally worked within the system and implemented the social functioning model, that locates the 'problems' within the individual, turn around and look at people from a very different standpoint—as possessors of rights and not as 'people with problems'. The answer to these questions probably lies in adopting a participatory approach in all their endeavours. The participatory rights based programming should therefore seek to (a) address gaps and violations of rights, *e.g.* through the distribution of food aid, reunification of separated children, sexual exploitation; (b) strengthen structures and mechanisms, *e.g.* policy change, legislation development, institution building; and (c) strengthen communities and civil societies capacity to support rights. As the following figure shows, the rights based efforts are in two directions: strengthening the accountability of duty bearers and supporting right holders in demanding their rights. If right holders demand their rights from the duty bearers and duty bearers in turn fulfil their obligation towards the right holders, it is expected to lead to a change in the lives of the people, who would become more empowered and human rights would be realized.

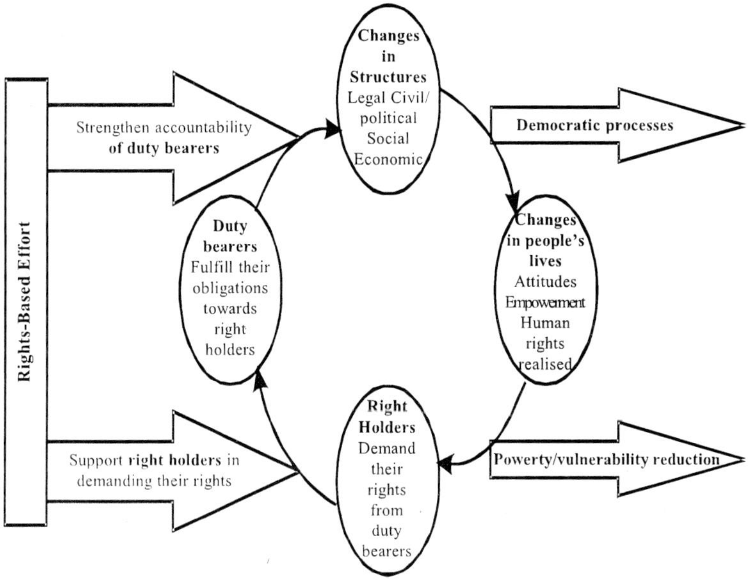

Source: Cecilia M. Ljungman, COWI, A Rights-Based Approach to Development

A rights based analysis seeks to identify patterns of poverty, powerlessness, social exclusion and discrimination in the communities. It goes beyond socio-economics, towards aspects of a society's social, cultural, legal and political dynamism. The main purpose is to capture the root causes of the perpetuation of poverty, exclusion, discrimination and power relations that sustain inequity. The problem analysis seeks to understand whose rights and what rights are not being realised or violated. This can be made more relevant by disaggregating data according to gender, caste, class etc. to identify which categories of people do not have access to their rights. In order to determine what immediate, underlying and structural obstacles there are to realising rights, we need to examine social, cultural, legal and administrative frameworks, and how people's claims are processed by authorities in the different arenas of negotiation. A rights-based analysis must necessarily identify responsible duty-bearers. Not only does this include the state at different levels, it also comprises the identification of other duty-bearers in society, including family, the community, corporate actors, etc. The capacities and resources of the duty-bearers to fulfil their duties also need to be assessed.

Challenges in Applying a Rights-based Approach: There are considerable and numerous challenges to effectively implement a rights-based approach to development. They relate to the inadequacy of state legal apparatuses, inconsistencies between law and practice and poor awareness of human rights among state actors and citizens. Inspite of many states having ratified the various human rights instruments, they have yet to find place in the domestic legal framework—which may often contain laws that are breaching human rights principles. Many poor countries do not have an effectively operating judicial system. In addition, citizens may be unaware of their rights and responsibilities as citizens, making it impossible for them to claim their rights and actively participate in democratic processes; and, the cost of engaging in the legal processes, including opportunity cost may be often too high for poor people, thus deterring them from approaching the courts.

It is therefore important to undertake advocacy and provide technical assistance to ensure that a state's formal laws comply with the human rights regime. Also, building the capacity of the justice and law sector and raising awareness of human rights among duty-bearers and rights-holders are of central importance.

Presently, there is little experience of applying rights-based approaches and insufficient practical guidance available. Most development practitioners have limited knowledge of the human rights and associated instruments requires a systematic educational effort within the development community. However, the idea of human rights has gained currency and cannot be replaced.

Participatory Attitudes: Working in a participating manner requires not only a paradigmatic shift but also an attitudinal change in the development workers. A few of the attitudes that need to be cultivated to make for effective participatory work include:

- The recognition that every idea counts and everybody's view counts: It is important to recognize that different individuals and groups have—according to their respective background—different perceptions and thus assess situations differently, which then leads them to different actions. This applies to all—including facilitators and promoters of participatory processes. Everyone's view is coloured with interpretation, bias and prejudice, which means that there are multiple descriptions and interpretations of real world phenomena, events and actions. Accepting this fact leads to an understanding that everyone is different and can offer important contributions to the participatory process, as their views which may look worthless or provocative at first sight, can complement those of others. Local communities are knowledgeable and have a vast repository of experience. It is important to take into consideration that different views only help to enlarge understanding.

- Adopting a learning attitude: All concerned and involved in the participatory processes should adopt a learning attitude, through which they learn from the persons/groups they are working with—rather than a teaching or preaching attitude. This 'learning attitude' can be enhanced by acknowledging persons/groups' experiences in, and knowledge of their own context and living conditions, by considering them as experts in dealing with their own situation and problems. The local communities have their own world view and capacity to analyse their problems and act. Their knowledge and experience are relevant for development purposes and are worthy of respect. The local communities are capable of rational decision making, implementing, monitoring and assessing, whether as a community, group, household or individuals. An outsider has an opportunity to learn from local communities about their lives and livelihoods with an appropriate attitude and behaviour. Thus the role of a facilitator is to enhance the involvement of all concerned persons/groups by supporting processes (such as investigation, analysis and evaluation of problems, constraints and opportunities, and taking informed and timely decisions).
- Ensuring transparency: Participatory decision-making requires readiness to reach a 'win-win' compromise from

all sides. An atmosphere of mutual trust is the basis for compromise and constructive co-operation and transparency by all stakeholders is a basic requirement. Transparency helps to avoid hidden agendas and suspicion amongst different parties and thus to prevent situations in which all parties try to protect their own interests rather than finding the most suitable solution for all parties involved.

- Being flexible: Being open to other persons' ideas and opinions is often the most difficult aspect of participatory processes. Often, other person's views may be difficult to understand and contradictory or incompatible with one's own ideas and beliefs. Accepting this reality requires a high degree of flexibility, as well as courage to set aside for a moment one's own perception and neutrally follow the process, being ready to rethink and re-plan at any stage, if necessary.
- Questioning our values: Most development workers have their own set of assumptions and values about society and the nature of people, particularly, the marginalised and poor. Development workers need to question their own values and attempt to sync them with the larger ideology and values of the participatory approach.
- Offsetting biases: Facilitators need to offset certain traditional biases. For example, development work has very often suffered from a roadside bias-people tend to visit those villages and localities that are located on the roadside or connected by roads. Often gender bias also becomes evident when we only interact with men. People bias creeps in when we interact only with key persons in the area leaving out the common man. Time bias, which is visiting communities only at own convenient time rather than their convenient time is also one of the biases. Often, we visit communities only in the dry seasons and not during the problematic rainy season.
- Help local communities to do their own analysis: Development workers are often impatient and tend to take over processes from the local community. They attempt to do things for the community that the community should

be doing itself. This negates the whole purpose of following a participatory approach. There is need to help the local communities do their own analysis, as their interpretation of data and analysis etc. would be dependent on the earlier data that they only possess. Also, when local communities do their own analysis, they would bring in their own interpretation of reality, from their own perspective.

- Gaining bird's eye view as well as worm's eye view: Development workers and facilitators have been fascinated with a broad birds eye view for long. There is an erroneous assumption that a macro, birds eye view helps to put things in perspective. Yet, it is important to have a worm's eye view of the issue too. A bird's eye view is an aggregated view, subsuming a lot of differences and differentness among people, whereas a worm's eye view would bring out the unique situation of each population group, interest group, or locale.
- Put poor people first of all: It is important to recognize that the participatory approach is about people and people only. This approach seeks to put the interests, perceptions, attitudes and behaviour of the people above everything. People have to be given importance over processes, targets and achievements. During the course of implementation of a project, participatory processes may reveal the real interests of the people that may sometimes be at odds with those of the project. In such cases, it is the people who should prevail and not the project.
- Role reversal: Four reversals have been identified in participatory learning and action:

  * The reversal of frames: A shift from the categories and values of outsiders to those of local people, enabling them to help define the frame of investigation.
  * Reversals of modes: The greater use of group work rather than individual informants; the use of visual rather than verbal techniques; and using comparison as a means of finding out quantitative data rather than direct measurement;

* Reversals of relations: Establishing rapport and involvement with local people rather than reserve and distance from them;
* Reversals of power: Enabling local people to enhance their own capacities for finding out and using and improving their own knowledge, rather than investigators extracting information for use elsewhere.

Key Principles: While applying participatory methods and tools, certain key principles have to be followed. A few of them are elaborated below:

- Leading to action and debate about change: Participatory processes lead to debates about desired changes in existing conditions and hence changes in the perceptions of the actors and their readiness to contemplate action. The process of joint analysis and dialogue helps to define desired changes and seeks to motivate people to implement them. This action includes local institution-building and strengthening, thus increasing the capacity of people to initiate collective self-help action aimed at improving their own futures.
- Iterative actions and tepwise analysis: Participation is an iterative process, which should continue throughout the project cycle. Decisions/agreements should be revisited periodically and checked for validity, and adjusted to changes that may have occurred in the conditions/situations/needs in the meantime. This implies that analytical processes should follow a stepwise procedure; to focus on general information gathering in the beginning, then on specific topics, and finally enter into a detailed (in-depth) analysis of local problems, needs and potentials. Additionally, the facilitation team should constantly review their findings in order to determine in which direction to proceed.
- Multiple perspectives/triangulation: Once the different points of view have been taken into consideration, the output of the analysis/discussion will provide a more

complete and accurate picture of the situation under review. Therefore, when trying to facilitate a participatory process, one should seek to mix team composition, tools and techniques, as well as sources of information/interest groups. In order to lend itself to understanding different perspectives, the participatory teams should be multi-disciplinary, with a good mix of gender, different backgrounds and skills, insiders and outsiders etc. They (the team) should experiment with a range of tools and techniques, including interviewing, mapping, diagramming, ranking, observing, discussing, and using secondary data etc. Also, while conducting the participatory exercises, it should be ensured that varied sources of information are contacted and included in the process. This could include population and interest groups like women and men, elders and youth, different socio-economic groups, different professions etc.

- Flexibility in applying instruments and choosing degree of precision: There is no a recipe nor blueprint on how to facilitate participatory processes. Methods and tools should not be used mechanically but should be context specific and appropriate to address the question or topic under discussion. The selection of a particular tool should also be determined by the specific characteristics of the society/ community/group the participation team is working with. The aim of participatory problem analysis is not to achieve absolute accuracy (one does not have to know/discuss everything), but an appropriate or adequate degree of precision. In order to determine what is 'adequate', facilitators should ask themselves "What kind of information is required, for what purpose, and how much information will people need for their analysis?"
- Visual sharing: Through visualization within a participatory process, participants have the opportunity to follow a discussion easier, especially illiterate people and people who join a session later than others. Maps, diagrams, rankings and other forms of visualization tools also promote consensual decision-making since everybody

is able to directly express their opinion on a chart or on the ground.

- Group Learning: Participatory workshops and other complex participatory processes are best facilitated by the use of interdisciplinary teams, since the complexity of most situations will only be revealed through group analysis and interaction, thus allowing for different experts to contribute.
- Self-critical Awareness: Promoters/facilitators of participatory processes have to be extremely careful to constantly analyze their own biases. This means to constantly reflect upon the phenomena they feel they have perceived, actually heard and observed and which they have already judged or interpreted.

An Overview of Participatory Approach

Behaviours and Attitudes	*Tools and Methods*	*Sharing and Partnership*
• Giving up control • Learning and listening • Open minded • History • Respecting differences • Motivation • Adaptability/flexibility and passion • Listening well/active listening • Speaking their languages and less academic • Informal rather than formal • Provide a comfortable environment that allows all present to participate fully and completely in all aspects of the dialogue	• Focus groups • Sorting, etc. exercises • Games • Mapping • Introductions • Wheel • Plain language • Visualization • Flexible, accessible and responsive to the needs and expectation of all participants, multidisciplinary and exciting to all • Use different learning styles—visual, auditory and kinesthetic • Building on past coping strategies to deal with challenges	• Exchange in knowledge • Engaging people in the process • Action outlet • Policy development based on findings • Discussing ideas • Building relationships/networks • Debrief (reflection) with participants • Identify problems together with the target group • Requires that at all stages of information sharing, decision making and reporting should be all inclusive

(contd)

(contd)

Behaviours and Attitudes	*Tools and Methods*	*Sharing and Partnership*
• Open minded • Respect • Group mentality—awareness of commonalities and differences • Belonging • Open to surprises • Researchers approach with humility	• Community consultation • Seasonal calendars • Time charts • Event books • Community mapping • All participants share in defining research questions • Object-oriented participatory planning (*e.g.* Zopp)	• Shared interest in research • All people/participants have input/participate • Returning results of research • Build group atmosphere/participation • Knowledge/learning is exchanged between all participants • Respect for local knowledge • Identifying group's objective

Source: Participatory Development Forum (2006).

Auxiliary and supplemental skills in participatory community work: If community work is to proceed in a rights based perspective, advocacy as a strategy becomes one of the logical choices. Advocacy means amplifying the voice of the marginalised and voiceless with a view to influencing policies that impact on their lives. In order to effectively carry out advocacy, often, organizations have to build up alliances and partnerships, which bring out the need to understand the process of networking. A recent development in the area of people's participation and responsive governance is the concept of social audit. In addition, there is need to appreciate the finer nuances of participatory project management and participatory research too.

Advocacy: As mentioned earlier, advocacy as a strategy becomes one of the logical choices in an rights based work. It is imperative that development workers develop the understanding and skills required for effective advocacy work. Advocacy is perceived as a systematic process of influencing public policies. It is understood that while policy change is necessary, it is not sufficient to transform the structures, attitudes, and values that are at the root of societal inequities and injustice. Instead, a more people-centered approach focused on social transformation is needed. People-centered advocacy is an array of well thought of organised actions, aimed at influencing policies, societal attitudes, and the socio-political processes that enable and empower the marginalised to speak for themselves. The purpose of people centered advocacy is social transformation through the realisation of civil, political, economic, social, and cultural human rights.

As Samuel J. (2002) puts it, 'people-centered advocacy is about mobilising the politics of the people to ensure that the politics of the state is accountable, transparent, ethical, and democratic.' It is a mode of social and political action. Following a rights based approach to social transformation and change, it looks upon people not as passive beneficiaries or charity seekers of the state or government. Rather the people have the right to demand a just and equitable social system. Citizens constitute a state and own it; thus the state apparatus has to be transparent and accountable to the people. People centered advocacy therefore stands against the societal violations of human rights.

The span of people centered advocacy is large—from grass-roots activism to influencing social policy. It attempts to create an organic link between the gains at the grassroots and macro level policy change. Through its micro level activism, it seeks to enhance the participation of the people in social policy formulation and implementation. People-centered advocacy goes beyond the old social action model in that, instead of advocating on behalf of the marginalised and voiceless, it seeks to empower the marginalised to articulate for themselves. As people-centered advocacy works on the values of social justice and human rights, it seeks to challenge the unjust and unequal power relations in society.

Three integrative principles of people centered advocacy, viz participation, communication and legitimacy have been identified by Samuel (2002). For him 'participation is not a mere strategy to manufacture consent, manipulate consensus or extract cheap labour. Participation is a principle based on an inclusive moral choice; participation means sharing power, legitimacy, freedom, responsibilities, and accountability. Participation is both a principle and means to include as many people as possible in the process of social change. Built on a deep respect for plurality, tolerance, and dissent, it also involves an ability to understand and appreciate differences. Transparency is a pre-requisite for true participation. In people-centred advocacy, participation is a crucial means to initiate, inform, and inspire change in all arenas of advocacy'. Communications become an important component in the people centered advocacy process. It is an attitude to share, reach out and speak. The communication elements in the process of people centered advocacy include Communicate to Convince; Convince to Change; Change to Commit and Commit to Convert to the cause. Also, advocacy communication needs to be consistent, continuous, creative, compelling, and convincing. For Samuel, legitimacy is an important component. Legitimacy has a moral-ethical-political connotation and is not something that can be assumed; rather it is acquired through values, attitudes, commitment etc. Connected to the perception of power, legitimacy is derived over a period of time through a series of actions. It is the sense of deep commitment, accountability, communicability, and action that help to derive legitimacy. It is both relative and dynamic, and fosters credibility. Each arena of advocacy demands a particular type of legitimacy (2002).

A common confusion in the development of advocacy strategy is the difference between "strategy" and "tactics." Tactics are specific actions—circulating petitions, writing letters, staging a protest—that are the building blocks of advocacy. Strategy is something larger, an overall map that guides the use of these tools toward clear goals. Strategy is a hard-nosed assessment of where you are, where you want to go, and how you can get there. The Advocacy institute has outlined nine questions as part of the strategic planning process for advocacy (2002).

(1) What do we want? (Goals): Advocacy efforts have to

begin by identifying the goals, both long term as well as short term. Goals can also be classified further into whether they are content goals, *i.e.,* whether they seek to effect a change in the policies, or whether they are process goals, where the process of building solidarity among the community may be more important.

(2) Who can give it to us? (Audiences; key players; or power-holders): The next step to be taken in the advocacy effort is to identify the sources from where these goals can be leveraged. They could be those who have the actual authority to deliver the goods, in the formal institutions and authorities like legislators and corporators etc. Another source could be those who are in a position to influence the formal authorities. These could include the media and other key constituencies. In both cases, an effective advocacy effort requires a clear sense of who these audiences are and what access or pressure points are available to move them.

(3) What do they need to hear? (Messages): In order to reach out to the different audiences, persuasive messages have to be designed. Often, these messages need to be tailored differently for different audiences, but without compromising on the truth. In most cases, advocacy messages will have two basic components: an appeal to what is right and an appeal to the audience's self-interest.

(4) Who do they need to hear it from? (Messengers): Communicator has an important role to play as the same message can have a different impact depending on who is communicating. The most credible communicators need to be identified for each section of the audience. These could be experts, or authentic voices. However, we need to provide the messengers with as much information as possible so that they are able to make a strong case in a convincing manner.

(5) How can we get them to hear it? (Delivery): Advocacy messages can be delivered in a variety of ways. They could be through lobbying or could be direct action in the form of protest marches or sit-ins etc. There is no one best method—depending on the situation, an effective way or mix of ways has to be identified, evaluated and then an appropriate mix adopted.

(6) What do we have? (Resources): What resources do we have to build up our advocacy strategy on? This could include the activities of similar advocacy organization or efforts made by others, or a network that already exists, the capacity of the people, their information level etc. Advocacy efforts do not always have to start from a scratch, they can start by building whatever is available.

(7) What do we need to develop? (Gaps): With information on what resources are available, it is important to now examine what resources are missing. This could mean that more information is required on the issue, more alliances have to be built, more messengers need to be co-opted etc. Also, capacity of the organization or alliances also needs to be examined and in cases of shortfall, built up.

(8) How do we begin? (First steps): The most effective way to move the strategy forward needs to be identified. What are some potential short term goals or projects that would bring the right people together, symbolize the larger work ahead and create something achievable that lays the groundwork for the next step?

(9) How do we tell if it's working? (Evaluation): As discussed earlier, there is need to keep track of the course that the effort is taking. There may be need to re-evaluate strategies at various stages. We may need to ask ourselves—are we aiming the right audience? are we reaching them effectively? It is important to be able to make mid-course corrections and to discard those elements of a strategy that don't work once they are actually put into practice.

As is described in the table on issue life cycle, any advocacy issue has a life span and life cycle. It has been broken down into six identifiable stages, viz, birth, childhood, adolescence, adulthood, maturity and renewal. The various characteristics of the issue through its stages are explained in the column on characteristics. Additionally, the nest steps to be taken at each stage and actions to be taken are also described.

Issue's Life Cycle Stage and the Next Steps for Advocacy

Stage	*Characteristics*	*Next Steps*	*Actions to Take*
Birth	A new demand, issue, idea, or proposal takes form. It is not yet recognized by others.	**Build support** to advance the idea.	• Define the issue, as well as its impact on people and communities • Raise the issue through protest or other ways to exert pressure
Childhood	The issue or idea begins to acquire networks of support.	**Nurture** the issue or idea.	• Move "from protest to politics": engage in public argument and generate possible solutions • Build alliances • Work with the media • Analyze policy alternatives
Adolescence	The issue or idea advances through the early stages of decision-making. It takes on more importance and legitimacy, gaining champions within influential institutions and among some key decision makers. Others begin to contribute ideas about different paths to the desired result.	**Focus the discussion** in ways that aren't divisive, but rather advance the issue towards a decision.	• Work inside the corridors of power to negotiate compromises with decision makers • Exert steady pressure from outside to maintain political will to take action
Adulthood	The issue reaches a resolute decision.	**Plan in detail** for a sufficient workability.	• Analyze the budget to make sure the final solution has the commitment and resources needed to be effective

(*contd.*)

(*contd.*)

Stage	*Characteristics*	*Next Steps*	*Actions to Take*
Maturity	The idea is implemented.	**Monitor and evaluate actions** for effectiveness.	• Work closely with constituents to monitor the solution's impact • Generate data and give feedback to decision makers
Renewal	Implementation is evaluated further.	**Improve implementation** and **search for broader applicability.**	• Review progress and determine the next action steps

Source: Advocacy Institute, 2004 Washington, DC

The table given below draws together four possible dimensions of success in advocacy work. It is not suggested that these have equal weighting in every situation or for every type of issue. However, for most advocacy issues, a number of these will be important. Each of these dimensions of success is complex in itself and may require different methods for monitoring and evaluating change. However it is important that these dimensions are not seen in isolation of each other as success in one dimension can influence progress in another (Chapman, J., 2002).

Framework for understanding possible outcomes and impact of advocacy and campaigning work

Dimension of work	*Intermediate objectives*	*Longer-term objectives*
1. Policy change	• Increased dialogue on an issue • Raised profile of issue • Changed opinion (whose?) • Changed rhetoric (in public/private) • Change in written publications	• Changed policy • Change in legislation • Change in resource allocation • Policy/legislation change implemented *(and in the very long term)* • Positive change in people's lives as a result of the policy/ legislation change

(*contd.*)

(*contd.*)

Dimension of work	*Intermediate objectives*	*Longer-term objectives*
2. Strengthening civil society by working with individual organisations and net works	• Change in individual members' skills, capacity, knowledge and effectiveness? • Change in individual civil groups' capacity, organisational skills, effectiveness? • Greater synergy of aims/ activities in networks/ movements • Change in collaboration, trust or unity of civil society groups	• Increased effectiveness of civil society work • Civil groups active in influencing decision makers in ways that will benefit poor people • Civil groups monitoring implementation of policies/ programmes. • Partnerships and networks effective and sustainable
3. Supporting people centred policy making	• Greater awareness of individual rights and the power systems that with-hold rights • Change in local people's skills, capacity, and knowledge to mobilise and advocate on their own behalves • Increased reporting of right violations • Existence of systems to monitor rights • Claims made by CBOs for enforcing rights	• Improved access to basic rights such as health, housing, water, food, non-discrimination
4. Enlarging democratic space or the space in which civil society groups can effectively operate in society	• Greater freedom of expression • Greater acceptance/recognition of civil groups • Existence for a civil groups to input into a wider range of decisions • Increased legitimacy of civil society groups	• Increased participation of civil society groups in influencing decisions • Change in accountability and transparency of public institutions

Developed by Ros David from IDR, 1999, quoted in Chapman, J, (2002)

Networking: As mentioned earlier, one of the key ways of functioning of NGOs today is through networks and networking. As Karl M. (1999) elaborates, networks and networking enables people and organisations to:

- Enhance and deepen critical thinking and creativity;
- Address global problems through global action;
- Transcend isolation and strengthen local action;
- Increase peoples potential for social and political action;
- Respect diversity while working together;
- Link local organising efforts and structures to international ones;
- Be inclusive;
- Be flexible and respond quickly to new situations; and
- Accomplish together more than can be done as individuals or single organisations alone.

Today, networking has become a conscious form of organising among NGOs who seek to influence the social, economic and political forces that shape peoples lives and surroundings. The need for networking arises because NGOs and other groups require information on what is happening on a particular issue across the nation or even internationally. Networks help to process and disseminate information across its membership that may be very wide spread. As a result, all interested get to have the key information that is required for analysis and possible action. Often networks generate and share information, experiences, ideas, views and strategies through publishing newsletters, setting up resource centres, developing information dossiers, setting up email groups, organising dissemination seminars and conferences etc. Networking thus widens the outreach and helps to build up a multiplier effect in terms of impact and public discourse.

Often, a critical incident, like a major human rights violation or a pressing need, mobilizes people and groups who feel the need to act. They may want to advocate for particular positions on specific issues and take the form of policy analysis, lobbying etc. A network is often triggered through this process and groups start getting mobilized and respond through writing of petitions, protest marches, sit-ins, candle light marches, etc. in public places so as to attract the attention of the masses as well as that of the government. These groups may later decide to form coalitions, alliances or networks to continue working together on such and similar issues. Networks may also often need to build and strengthen the capacity of its constituents and may organize trainings, workshops, cross-visits for developing campaigning, lobbying and strategizing skills. This is often the first stage in the development of a network. In this stage, a few organizations that are better placed in terms of skills and resources take the lead and others pitch-in. The network at this stage is in an informal shape and loose. The network may decide to formalize its existence by establishing a secretariat and making some funds available for skeleton staff. As the network expands, it may feel the need to formalize itself more and also, the other partners in the network may feel the need to have their voices heard and their views represented on the network. Thus some regional offices of the network are set up and adequate representation is ensured for all. Finally, it may develop a constitution, a charter, with clear paid membership for organizations and launch itself, independent of the promoting organizations. All networks do not last, only a few survive the initial enthusiasm and teething troubles in the initial phases. Networks that have a particular focus and supported by adequate funding stand a reasonable chance of surviving. For networks to be sustainable, it is important that they should serve a need, have a common cause and build up trust, both internally and externally (See Karl M, 1999).

Social Audit: A social audit is a way of measuring, understanding, reporting and ultimately improving an organization's social and ethical performance. A social audit helps to narrow gaps between vision/goal and reality, between efficiency and effectiveness. It is a technique to understand, measure, verify, report on and to improve the social performance of the organization.

Social auditing creates an impact upon governance. It values the voice of stakeholders, including marginalized/poor groups whose voices are rarely heard. Social auditing is taken up for the purpose of enhancing local governance, particularly for strengthening accountability and transparency in local bodies (www.fao.org/docrep). It is based on the principle that democratic local governance should be undertaken with the consent and understanding of all stakeholders. It is thus seen as a process and not an event.

Social audit has a number of advantages; it prepares the community to take up the responsibility for participatory local planning. It encourages local level democracy and community participation, particularly for the disadvantaged groups. As local level democracy, it promotes collective decision making and responsibility sharing. In turn, it helps in developing local human resources and social capital.

Social audit is undertaken mainly for the purposes of assessing the physical and financial gaps between needs and resources available for local development. It helps in creating awareness among beneficiaries and providers of local social and productive services. Through scrutiny of various policy decisions, keeping in view stakeholder interests and priorities, particularly of rural poor, it increases efficacy and effectiveness of local development programmes. In a way, social audit includes measures for enhancing transparency by enforcing the right to information in the planning and implementation of local development activities.

To be effective, the social auditor must have the entitlement and privilege to seek clarifications from the implementing agency about any decision-making, activity, scheme, income and expenditure incurred by the agency; consider and scrutinize existing schemes and local activities of the agency; and access registers and documents relating to all development activities undertaken by the implementing agency or by any other government departments (www.fao.org/docrep). This requires transparency in the decision-making and activities of the implementing agencies.

The Panchayat Raj Acts in most states in India, have given supervisory powers to the Gram Sabha to monitor the functioning of panchayat elected representatives and government functionaries, and examine the annual statement of accounts and audit reports. They are thus the most appropriate institutional level for social audit. A number of public documents listed below have to be open for social audit at the grassroots level;

(a) All budget allocations, beneficiary lists, muster rolls, bills, vouchers, accounts, etc. must be available for public scrutiny.
(b) All applications for licenses/permits and certificates issued by local self-government institutions must have a serial number. Registers indicating date of application and date of clearance in each case should be available for reference by any applicant. If possible, copies should be publicly displayed.
(c) Public assessment of tax, exemptions, grants, etc., to ensure there are no complaints of undue preferential treatment.

Several states have declared all Gram Panchayat plan documents related to beneficiary selection, budget cost estimates, etc. to be public documents. A daily notice to be posted at the site of all development works, lists names of workers, wages paid, cost and quantities of material, transport charges, etc. Social audit becomes a potent weapon once it is combined with the Right to Information Act, passed recently.

Participatory Project Management: The Logical Framework Approach (LFA) is a planning and management tool, developed in the USA in the 1970s. In the Logical Framework Approach a development project is viewed as a causally linked sequence of events. It is assumed that if the inputs are available, then the activities will take place, if the activities take place, then the outputs will be produced, if the outputs are produced, then the purpose will be achieved and in the long run, this will contribute to the fulfilment of the goal. The Logical Framework is developed step-by-step, starting with the analysis, followed by planning and designing the project.

Analysing the Situation

Participation Analysis
Problem Analysis
Objectives Analysis
Alternatives Analysis

Designing the Project

Project Elements
External Factors
Indicators

Using LFA ensures that fundamental questions are asked and weaknesses are analysed, in order to provide decision-makers with better and relevant information. It helps in systematic and logical analysis of the inter-related key elements of the project. LFA helps in improved planning by highlighting the linkages between project elements and external factors. Also, using LFA provides a better basis for monitoring and analysis of the effects of the project. Once the project is converted into a project planning matrix through LFA, it helps in developing a common understanding and better communication between decision makers and other parties involved in the project.

Indicative Project Planning Matrix as per the Logical Framework

	Objectively Verifiable Indicators	*Means of Verification*	*Assumptions/External Factors*
GOAL The higher level objective towards which the project is expected to contribute	Measures (direct or indirect) to verify to what extent the goal is fulfilled	Where/how to find the information	Important events, conditions or decisions necessary for sustaining objectives in the long run
PURPOSE The effect which is expected to be achieved as the result of the project	Measures (direct or indirect) to verify to what extent the goal is fulfilled	Where/how to find the information	Important events, conditions or decisions outside the control of the project which must prevail for the development objective to be attained
OUTPUTS The results that the project management should be able to guarantee	Measures (direct or indirect) to verify to what extent the goal is fulfilled	Where/how to find the information	Important events, conditions or decisions outside the control of the project management, necessary for the achievement of the immediate objective
ACTIVITIES The activities that have to be undertaken by the project in order to produce the outputs	**INPUTS** Goods and services necessary to undertake the activities. Resource inputs/costs		Important events, conditions or decisions outside the control of the project management, necessary for the production of the outputs

However, the LFA is not without its shortcomings. When objectives and externalities are emphasized, rigidity tends to set in. As an analytical tool, the LFA is policy neutral on such questions as income distribution, access to resources, cost and feasibility of strategies etc. It has also been criticized for being too managerial and treating people as targets and objects rather than subject. However, participatory concerns can be built into the logframe and PRA processes can be applied very early on involving the poor and marginalised in their own analysis of their needs and priorities. LFA should not be treated as an end in itself; rather it should be viewed as a means of achieving the desired objective. All aspects of the logframe can be developed with community participation. As the following figure, developed in Sri Lanka, describes, participatory concerns can be built into the process so as to ensure that the community concerns are the key determinants of the development process.

As is evident from the figure, step 1 of the situational analysis, participation analysis, would include participatory concerns such as who are the stakeholders, what stake do they have and how do they interact with the other stakeholders, that can be addressed through use of brainstorming, Venn diagrams or semi-structured interviews. Step 2 of the situational analysis, problem analysis, would include participatory concerns such as whose problems count? What are the causes and consequences and what is the reality? Whose priorities count? How does the local community perceive? These concerns can be addressed through the use of techniques and tools like the social mapping, resource mapping, seasonal charts, livelihood profiles and wealth, well-being ranking, matrix ranking and pair wise ranking.

Step 3 of the situational analysis, objectives analysis would include participatory concerns such as whose objectives or aspirations are to be taken into account? What are they? What is to be achieved in the short term and long term? These can be addressed through the use of participatory methods like the brainstorming, impact diagramming, semi-structured interviews. In step 4 of the situational analysis, alternative analysis, participatory concerns such as whose options and what? Who shares the benefits? are addressed through matrix scoring and options assessment. Similarly, in the Project Planning Matrix (or the Logframe), under the summary of objectives, participatory concerns like whose reality counts? What needs to change? Who decides?, etc. are addressed by participatory exercises and tools like the wealth and well-being ranking, livelihood profiles, mapping, impact diagrams and semi-structured interviews. In

FIG. 4: LINKING PRA TO LFA: ADDRESSING PARTICIPATORY CONCERNS

Participatory Concerns	PRA tools/techniques for generating information	Information needs for planning	LFA Steps
Whoare the stakeholders? What stoke do they have? How do primary stakeholders interact with the secondary	• Brainstorming • Venn diagrams by primary stakeholders • Semi-structured	• Identification of stakeholder groups/ individuals/institutions • Problems faced	**Situation analysis** Step 1 Participations analysis
Whose problems count? What are they? What are the cause and consequences?	• Social map • Resource map • Seasanal charts • Livelihood profiles • Wealth and well-being	• Problems, issues and concerns of villagers • Causes and effects • Issues related to project	**Situation analysis** Step 2 Problem analysis.
Whose priorities count? How does the local community perceive?	• Matrix ranking • Pair-wise ranking	• Criteria for prioritising problems • Problem prioritisation	(Situation analysis Step 2)
Whose objectives/ aspirations? What are they? What is to be achieved short?	• Brainstorming • Impact diagramming	Strategies and options proposed/desired by the community to overcome the problem situation	**Situation analysis** Step 3 Objectives analysis
Whose options and what? Who shares the benefits?	• Matrix sca\oring • Options assessment	• Criteria for assessing options • Alternative strategies/ options available	**Situation analysis** Step 4 Alternative Analysis
Whose reality counts? What needs to change? Who decides?	• Wealth and well-being ranking • Livelihood profiles • Mapping, impact	Development of project concept, vision, mission, results, activities	**Project/ Programme** planning Matrix (PPM) Summary of Objectives
How do we measure change/impact? Who impact? Who share	Base/post-project information derived from: • Wealth and well-being ranking • Livelihood profiles	Indicators that would capture and measure changes anticipated through interventions	**Project/PPM** Objectively Verifiable Indicators (OVIs)
Who has the information? Who needs to know?	Participatory Monitoring and Evaluation (PM&E) charts using PRA tools	Sources of information for impact monitoring. Who should do it? For whom? In what form? Records?	**Project/PPM** Means of Verification (MoVs)
Whose power/influence/ behaviours/attitudes	• Power relations • Historical time lines • Seasonal charts • Trend lines	Attitudes/behaviours, factors, processes, trends, natural hazards/disaster, etc., outside the control of the community/project	**Project/PPM** Important assumptions External Factors
Who does what and when? Who initiates? Who supports? Who commands?	• Brainstroming • SSI • Seasonal charts • Venn diagram	The appropriate activities/ sub-activities, time periods and capable groups/ institutions and persons for project/programme	Action, plan/Operator plan/Activities/ Sub-activities/Time frame/ Responsibilities.

Source: Samaranayake M, (2001).

the next column under the Objectively Verifiable Indicators, participatory issues like how do we measure change or impact? Whose impact? Who shares the benefits? are addressed by base/post project information derived from wealth and well-being ranking, livelihood profiles, mapping, impact diagrams and semi-structured interviews. Means of verification are addressed by who has the information? Who needs to know and monitor through the use of tools like participatory monitoring and evaluation and other PRA tools and visuals. Under the column on important assumptions/external factors, participatory interests like whose power/influence/behaviour/attitudes matter are dealt with through the use of PRA tools like historical time lines, seasonal charts, trend lines and key event analysis. Lastly, the action plan or the operational plan is built by addressing participatory concerns like who does what and when? Who initiates? Who supports? Who commands access? by brainstorming, semi-structured interviews, seasonal charts and Venn diagrams.

Fig. 5: Linking PRA to Community Work

Steps	*Methods*
1. **Rapport building:** Establishing confidence) with the community.	Direct observation field survey/learn from "them" Semi-structured individual interviews Key informant interviews focused group interviews *Appropriate place and time selection* *Active involvement of participants especially shy observers and listeners* *Restraint over dominant respondents* *Basic set of open-ended questions.*
2. **Community profiling:** Developing community map to assess its resources and needs.	Community resource mapping Community social mappingTrend lines Well being analysis Mobility mapping Seasonal calendar Daily activity chart Cash flow diagram

(*contd.*)

(contd.)

Steps	*Methods*
3. **Prioritization of problems, violations and issues:** Assessing the magnitude and gravity of problems, violations & issues and prioritizing them accordingly.	Pair wise ranking Preference or priority ranking Chapatti diagram Root-branch (cause-effect) diagram
4. **Strategy development:** Preparing a strategic analysis with aims, objectives and processes.	Problem analysis chart Preliminary community action plan Stakeholder Venn diagram
5. **Formation of action nucleus:** Facilitating the formation of groups and working towards their sustainability and effectiveness.	Assortment of people into groups based on categories of age, gender, socio-economic status or proximity. Leader Selection: ***How*** *Consensus* Voting ***When*** Rotation basis Regular frequency
6. **Conflict resolution:** Working over intra, inter group and organization conflict and confrontation.	Force Withdrawal Accommodation Compromise Consensus
7. **Advocacy and Networking:** Collaborating with other agencies and resources.	Co-operation Sharing goal and aspiration Action plan execution
8. **Organisational development and management:** Managing resources, staff and funds	Project Planning matrix Gantt Chart Project cash flow charts Cost-benefit analysis *Technical analysis* *Financial analysis*
9. **Monitoring and Evaluation:**	Planned Vs Achieved charts Gantt Charts Self monitoring and appraisal charts Focused Group Discussions. Key informant interviews *Locally developed indicators.* *Joint evaluation of the project.* *Immediate sharing of results.*
10. **Role transformation (phasing out or withdrawal):** Withdrawing from the group and community and making it self-dependent.	

Various authors in the field of community work have described it as a process with clear cut steps and stages. A participatory rights based approach to community work would require recalibration of the stages that have been propounded earlier. The table on linking PRA with community work attempts to bring out the participatory concerns at each stage of community work and what tools and methods can be used in the process to make community work more participatory and rights based. As can be seen from the table, community work has been divided into ten stages viz, rapport building, community profiling, prioritization of problems, violations and issues, strategy development, formation of action nucleus, conflict resolution, advocacy and networking, organisational development and management, monitoring and evaluation, and role transformation. At each stage, the participatory concerns can be addressed through the use of PRA methods, tools and techniques.

At the rapport building stage which includes establishing relationship (including trust, confidence) with the community, PRA tools like direct observation, field survey/learn from "them", semi-structured individual interviews, key informant interviews and focused group interviews can be used to establish rapport. It is important that appropriate place and time selection is made and active involvement of participants especially shy observers and listeners should be ensured. Also there may be need to exercise some degree of restraint over dominating respondents.

At the stage of community profiling, a mapping is done of the social structure as well as resources to have a better understanding of the dynamics of the community. PRA tools like community resource mapping, community social mapping, trend lines, well-being analysis, mobility mapping, seasonal calendar, daily activity chart, and cash flow diagram can be used.

In the next stage of prioritization of problems, the main task is the assessment of the magnitude and gravity of problems, violations & issues and prioritizing them accordingly. At this stage, PRA tools like pair wise ranking, preference or priority ranking, chapatti diagram, and root-branch (cause-effect) diagram can be used.

The next stage in participatory community work is the stage of strategy development. At this stage a strategic analysis is conducted that clearly delineates the aims, objectives and processes. PRA tools like the problem analysis chart, stakeholder Venn diagram and preliminary community action plan prove to be of much use.

In order to carry forward the process of participatory community work, action nucleus is formed in the community. This is the next stage in which facilitation of the formation of groups and working towards their sustainability and effectiveness is undertaken. PRA tools can be used to categorise people into groups based on groups of age, gender, socio-economic status or proximity. Groups would pass through the stages of orientation (forming), conflict (storming), collaboration (norming), productivity (performing) and changing (transforming). Decisions on how leaders have to be selected, whether through consensus or through voting; when and the duration of their leadership, whether on a rotation basis or otherwise, have to be taken.

As with any human process, participatory community work can also encounter conflicts. The next stage of community work is the resolutions of conflicts, where there is need to work over intra, inter group and organization conflict and confrontation. PRA tools can be useful in working out the best possible solutions, like force, withdrawal, accommodation, compromise or consensus.

As the process continues and work expands, community work reaches the stage where some kind of advocacy and networking is required. Organisations need to collaborate with other agencies and resources. PRA tools for enhancing co-operation, developing shared goal and aspirations and action plan execution can be used at this stage.

With growing complexity in work, there arises a need to be systematic and work towards organisational development and management. PRA tools like the project-planning matrix, gantt chart, project cash flow charts, cost-benefit analysis, technical analysis and financial analysis can be used to feed into the process.

Although monitoring and evaluation is listed as a step in the process, yet it is often an ongoing process throughout all stages. Tools like the planned vs achieved charts, gantt charts, self monitoring and appraisal charts, focused group discussions, and key informant interviews can be used. Care should be exercised to use locally developed indicators with joint evaluation of the project and immediate sharing of results.

The last stage is that of role transformation. In this the organization starts withdrawing from the group and community and attempts to make it self-dependent. There is transformation in the role that the community and organization have been undertaking and the community starts taking on more roles and responsibilities and the organization, less.

4

Participatory Tools and Methods

Different participatory methods use mapping as an integral tool. Mapping involves direct participation of the community. For mapping, visual elements are important, for which a range of symbols are used. Symbols help in visually portraying items and transferring mental pictures on to social maps and models. It facilitates the weak and voiceless to express their mental pictures and symbols. Participatory mapping helps to highlight different aspects of community life such as location of various castes in the community, resources, livelihoods, literacy etc. It helps to develop spatial drawing of the area on the ground or on paper by the local people to share and explain their locality and its various aspects to the outsiders.

Participatory mapping is done by the local people themselves, including all sections of the population. A few key informants lead the process and make the map, while other members of the community extend active support and give their inputs.

The potential of mapping in understanding the local community is immense. Such maps help in identifying resources of the community, types of houses, land use patterns, women headed households, ownership of assets etc. They empower the local community by helping create ownership of data by the local community, help in building rapport, understand uncharted territories and develop group participation and consensus in the community.

While mapping, it is important to note that a map denotes the perspective and world view that different groups in the community have of their own community. It is influenced by gender, caste, class, age, economic status, etc. Maps drawn by women have appeared to be significantly different from those drawn by men. Similar is the case with other groups too. This can be used by the facilitators to enhance their understanding of the finer nuances of community life.

Variants of participatory mapping can be social mapping, resource mapping, infrastructure mapping, health mapping, before/after mapping, then and now mapping, mobility mapping, livelihoods mapping etc.

A. Resource Map

Purpose

This tool is used to gather information about the resources, both natural and man-made present in a community (locality, colony, village, etc). It may be general or theme-based. It may include the local perceptions attached with the resources like their accessibility, ownership, control and utility.

The map may include the following:

Water bodies: pond, river, tank, canal, stream, etc.

Land: forest, cultivable (irrigated and monsoon-fed), plantation, grazing, etc.

Soil: type, slope, elevation, crop type, location, etc.

Infrastructure: road (motorable, metal, approach), electric poles, etc.

Special or community buildings: school, health centres, cemetery, religious buildings, chaupal, panchayat building, etc.

Shops, market area, open playing field, etc.

Process

A meeting is organized in which maximum participation of the community members is ensured. The participants must represent all sections of the community. Participants from all socio-economic, ethnic and religious groups including males and females should take part in preparing the community resource map.

In most situations, this is the first or starting tool and it aids in initiating a dialogue and concretizing relationship with the community. It creates a viable environment to discuss and explore forthcoming sensitive and complex issues.

The exercise can start by placing and labeling an item (*e.g.* pebble) as the central landmark or reference for the resources. Facilitating questions should be asked to bring out an elaborate and comprehensive map like categorization of resources vis-à-vis their importance, ownership, control and utility; what was the community originally like and how has it changed in terms of expansion, emergence and disappearance of dwelling areas and resources. Facilitators should clear their doubts and ask anything which is missed or unclear. In order to develop a preliminary plan and encourage participation, participants can be asked to draw resources that they find are missing or otherwise should be present to make an ideal community. The map can be drawn on ground and reproduced on chart paper or directly on paper.

Items

All the locally available materials like pebbles, stones, dry soil, mud, leaves, shoots, seeds, grains, flour, holi colour (gulal), etc. Chart paper, water colour, gum, tape, sketch pens, bold markers, etc.

Caution

Direction indicators (with reference to sun), community borders and resource boundaries should be near to precision.

Example

The map illustrates the resources, their location, relative distance and outline map of the community.

RESOURCE MAP

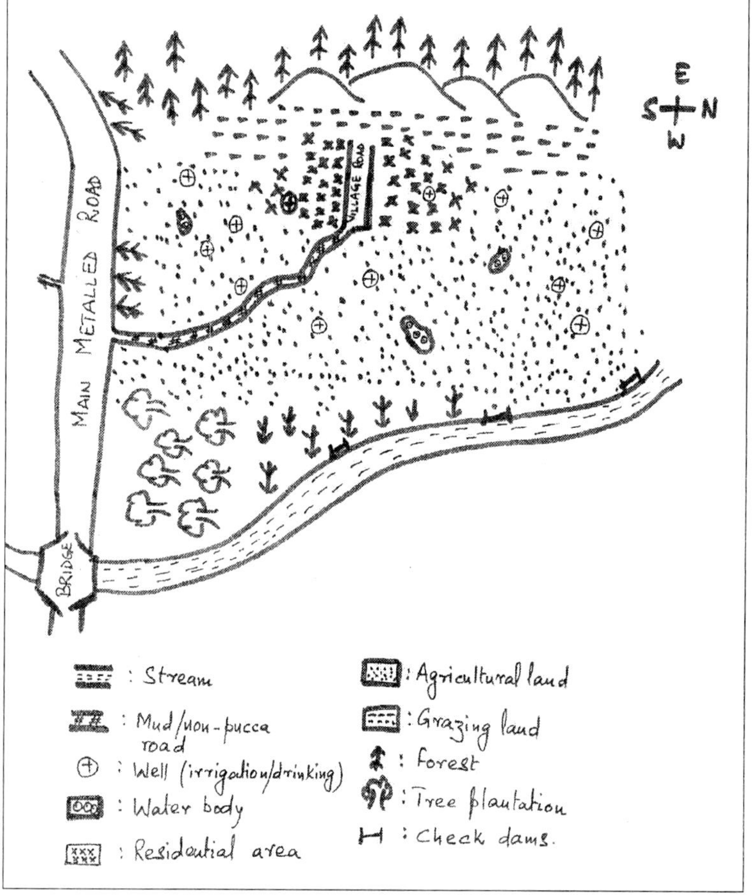

B. Social Map

Purpose

This tool is used to gather information and knowledge about the social structure of a community. It portrays social aspects of the locality, including demographic profile, social relationships and local perceptions on social issues.

It depicts the households, their types (based on socio-economic status, religion, ethnicity, and headship, concentration and location).

It also gives a preliminary idea about the stratification, inequity, social systems, dynamics, surviving strategies and mechanisms of the community members.

Process

A meeting is organised in which participation of key informants from the community is ensured. The informants must represent a cross-section of the population. The informants must have information on the households, social relationship and dynamics prevailing in the community. Males and females should participate in this exercise, either together or separately. The exercise can begin by locating a central landmark followed by each household in its reference on the map. This can be followed by formulating common, consensual criteria to do wealth ranking, asset survey and well-being analysis. Next, the households are labeled through different symbols like twigs, pebbles, colours, etc. to get pictorial idea about the socio-economic, religious, cultural and ethnic differences and commonality in the community. Besides, size of houses may also be symbolically shown on the map.

Direction indicators and borders must be precisely depicted. Facilitating questions like number of members, size of land (including backyard), livestock, dependents and earning members, nuclear or combined family (as per their perception) per household, concentration of houses based on ethnicity, religiosity, socio-economic status; migration, shifting from farming occupation can also be asked.

Items

All the locally available materials like pebbles, stones, dry soil, mud, leaves, shoots, twigs, seeds, grains, flour, holi colour (gulal), etc.

Chart paper, water colour, gum, tape, sketch pens, bold markers, etc.

Caution

This exercise may get sensitive and may not be as "apolitical" as the resource mapping exercise. While ranking, many respondents may project themselves as the most needy and aid-worthy and hence poor. So, triangulation can be done through secondary sources, non-participant observation and informal discussions.

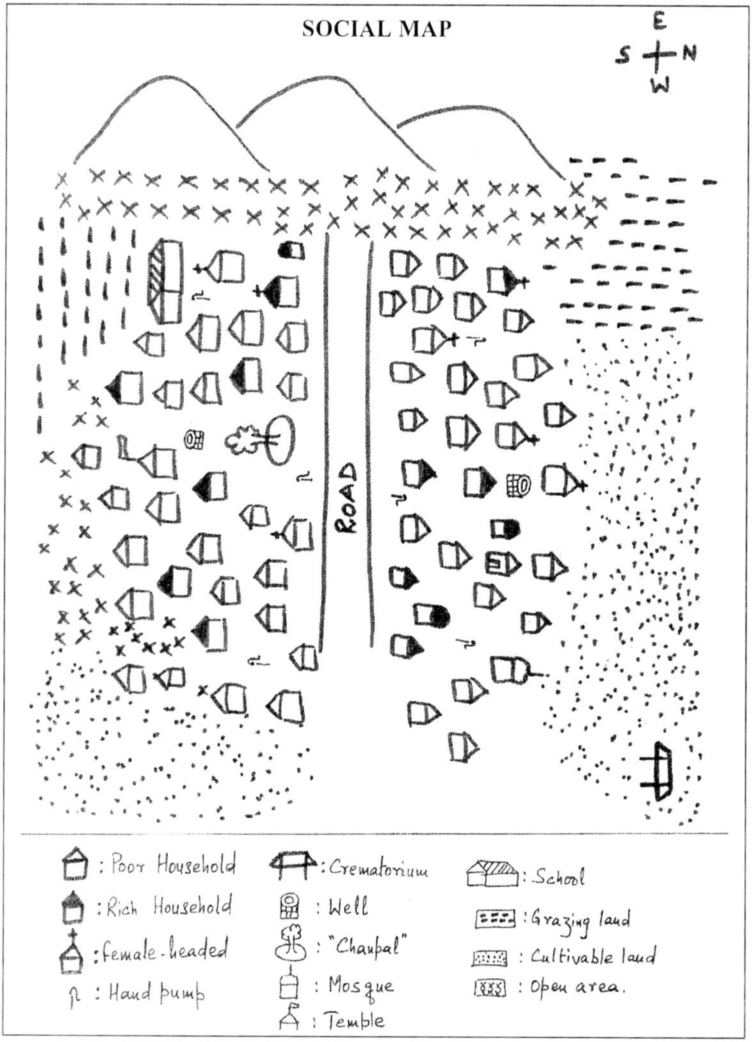

Note: Social map can be super-imposed over the resource map, if the need arises. For example, to see the geographical proximity of houses from key resources like water body, road, etc.

Example

The map illustrates the houses, their location and concentration, their relative position in the community vis-à-vis socio-economic status, headship, etc.

C. Transect Walk

Purpose

This tool provides in-depth information about the resources (natural and man-made) present in a community. It gives cross-sectional information about the selected area of community. It is conducted as a joint exercise with the key local informants when the area is surveyed and its resources, constituents and problems are observed, discussed, articulated and recorded during walk. It is a one-dimensional map and concentrates on a selected area. Transect can be done through straight or zigzag walking.

Process

Groups of key local informants are organised based on gender, age and economic status along with facilitators to conduct transect walk of the most important area of the community. Each group can concentrate on the area with a set agenda. For example, one group can prioritize water status, related infrastructure and amenities like wells, canal, surface water and other irrigation options and the other group prioritizes soil, crop type, plantation and deforestation.

Then the groups combine their research and findings on a transect map. The findings can be triangulated with the resource map which had given preliminary information on the available resources.

Facilitating questions can be asked to bring forth detailed information like what are the natural resources available in each zone of the area? what activities are done? what are the amenities and services available? what are the major issues (like control, ownership, disparity, etc) concerning that zone? what are the possible solutions?

Items

Notebooks, chart papers, sketch pens, bold markers and all the locally available materials like pebbles, stones, dry soil, mud, leaves, shoots, twigs, seeds, grains, flour, holi colour (gulal), etc.

Caution

Since it is an in-depth exercise and most of the information may be critical of overall community development or project formulation, so it is important that every information or data is recorded and "nothing" is missed.

It should be an exhaustive exercise and one should 'walk' for greater and sharper observation. There will be issues that may not have emerged during the resource map formulation. It is here that transects prove beneficial. The informants can take advantage by showing the zone rather than just describing them. It may provide facilitators scope for additional queries and topics to discuss.

Non-participants (group members) can also be asked to provide inputs, especially share sensitive informations like the problem of the area (inequity, disparity, diminishing resources, etc).

Example

The map depicts the combined transects that were produced by separate groups.

ZONE	Forest land	Agriculture land	Residential land	Arable land	Low land
SOIL TYPE	Sandy loam	Sandy and Clay loam	Sandy and sandy loam	Sandy loam	Clayey.
LAND USE	Gathering firewood; wild fruits	Producing wheat; millet and seasonal vegetable	Backyard crops	Rice ; Late millet; Sorghum : Seasonal vegetables	Paddy
TREE SPECIES	Wild trees; Sal ; Mango; Mahua ; Berry	Papaya; Guava; Jamun ; Mango.	Neem ; Tulsi ; Jackfruit	Jackfruit ; Papaya ; Guava ; Neem.	Mango ; jamun; Guava; Neem
SOIL EROSION	Slight	Medium/ High	High	High	Medium
WATER AVAILABI-LITY	Wild surface water ; stream	Well ; seepage tank	Well : Hand pump	Well	Pond ; Mini - streams
PROBLEM	Government restrication on collecting forest products	Lack of adequate irrigat-ion	Lack of sewage system	Soil fertility fast dwindling	Inadequate rainfall for past few years.

Transect walk

D. Well-Being Analysis

Purpose

This tool is used to compare the well-being of households based on certain criteria like land holding, livestock, type of house, gender status, health, education, social status etc. The criteria are arrived at through consensus. It can be used to analyse material (wealth ranking and asset survey), psychological as well as gender well-being.

This tool is a preliminary exercise to short list the would-be clients and the real poor or the poorest of the poor. It also tells us the perception of the local people about the concept of well-being

Process

A meeting of key informants from the community is organised. The informants must represent cross-section of the locality based on socio-economic status, gender and age. The informants must have information of the households. This exercise can be repeated a number of times for triangulation. To begin with, a list of head of households is prepared. Then the name of the head of each household is written on separate small, uniform sized cards. The households are then ranked accordingly through discussion and consensus. There can be three or four categories of classification: well-off, average, poor and poorest or happy, normal, sad and distressed. The categories may be represented by symbols or human faces made on paper. Facilitate respondents to enlist maximum criteria and not restrict to material well-being only. If necessary, prepare separate chart for psychological well-being. A table can be drawn where the categories (with corresponding set of criteria) can be put on horizontal axis and the households arranged under them.

Items

Notebooks, chart papers, sketch pens, bold markers, cards.

Caution

The respondents may become biased and project themselves as the poorest, so, triangulation is necessary.

Example

The chart illustrates the comparative well-being status of the households in a community.

Criteria	🙂	😐	🙁
Land Holding			
Water Resources			
No. of livestock			
House			
Credit or Debt			
Health of family members			
Children going to school			
Electronic equipments			
Earning members			
Relation with community			

Well-being Analysis

E. Seasonal Livelihood Calender

Purpose

It is a tool that helps us to track the changes in livelihood systems and income generation pattern of people in a year. This tool shows that how much work people have in different seasons. It informs in which season, income is less than expenditure and vice versa. It shows the seasonal variations and its effect on the lives of the people. It can be used to show the livelihood pattern of males and females separately.

Process

Separate focus groups of males and females are organized. The participants are asked to draw a horizontal line which represents a year. The respondents are asked to divide the line in months or seasons, as per their choice. The simplest way to start the exercise is by asking about the rainfall pattern. The participants can be asked to put symbol (like stone, twig or pebble) representing rain. The season or month with maximum rain will have maximum symbols. Similarly, other livelihood issues can be taken up like migration, non-farm activity, no or little work, income, expenditure, sources of food and income, food and fodder availability, etc. Facilitating questions like how expenditures and income vary over a year, which months are most and least productive can be asked.

Items

All the locally available materials like pebbles, stones, dry soil, mud, leaves, twigs, seeds, grains, flour, holi colour (gulal), dung, etc. Chart paper, gum, tape, sketch pens, bold markers, etc.

Caution

Normally, there should be difference if not fluctuation between seasons. If the villagers are not able to differentiate one season from another, facilitating questions should be asked.

Example

The following seasonal chart shows the activities of people in a year.

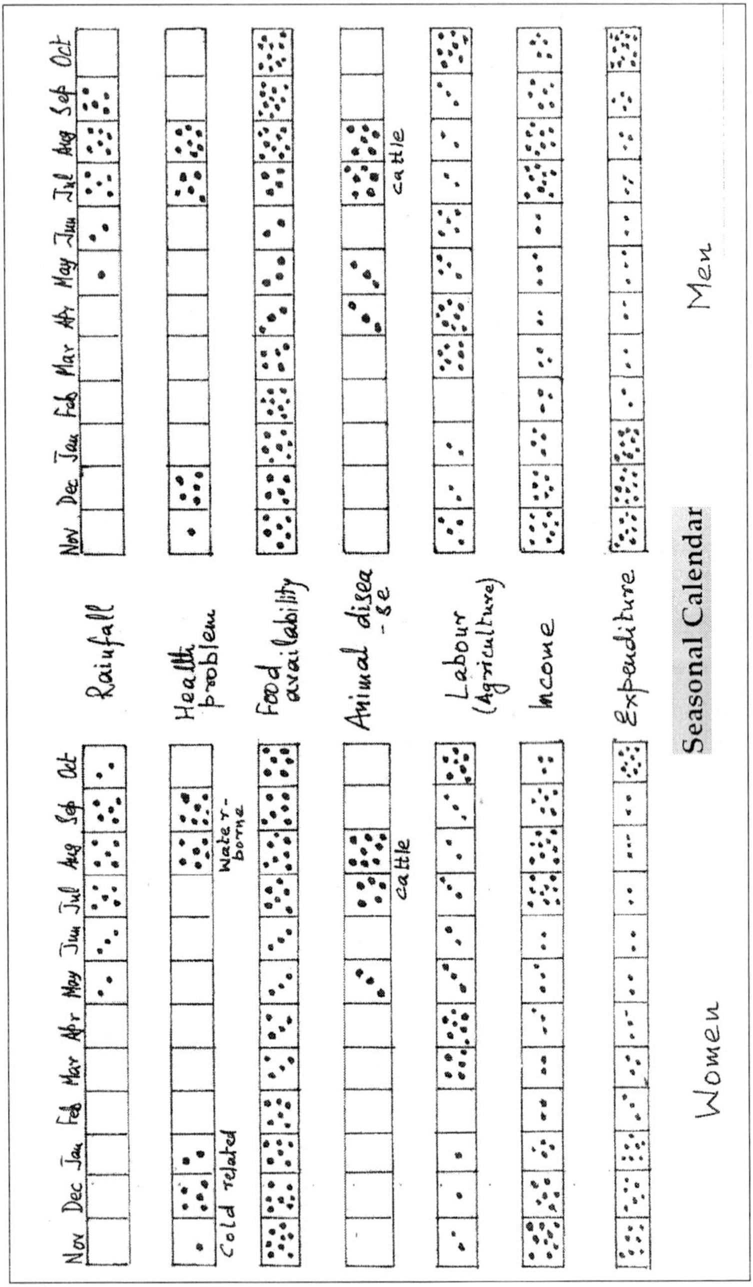

Seasonal Calendar

F. Daily Activity Clock

Purpose

This tool is used to gather information about the activities undertaken on a daily basis. It gives an idea about the work-load of different groups of people. This tool illustrates who is engaged for the maximum amount of time in a day, who has the least responsibility and work-load, who works for long stretches or whose work involves drudgery.

It also shows the kind of activities different types of people within a community are engaged in and how daily activities change according to season.

Process

Separate focus groups of males and females are organized. The respondents are explained that their daily activity routine is to be learnt and understood. A pie chart, representing a clock is drawn and the respondents are asked to enlist the activities they have done the previous day. Respondents may be asked or facilitated to represent the activity and the number of hours (or minutes, if needed) it took on the pie chart. Thus, the pie chart is completed with 24 hours of activity. If two or more activities are going together, they can be represented in the same space on the chart.

The previous day clock presents the current season. Likewise, respondents can be asked to draw activity clock for other seasons. Facilitating questions like who is the busiest? which part is most labour-intensive? who works more? who does maximum number of activities? etc., can be asked to understand the different roles of men, women, young, old, rich and poor.

Items

Chart paper, markers, compass or round object like bangle, ruler.

Caution

In case the respondents are not able to understand, team members can draw their own activity clock to facilitate them. The clock must represent an average day of the season. Leisure, sleeping, etc. are also activities and should not be missed. This gives the idea of who bears the maximum workload.

Example

The pie charts show the daily activity clock of men and women in different seasons.

Daily Activity Clock (Men)

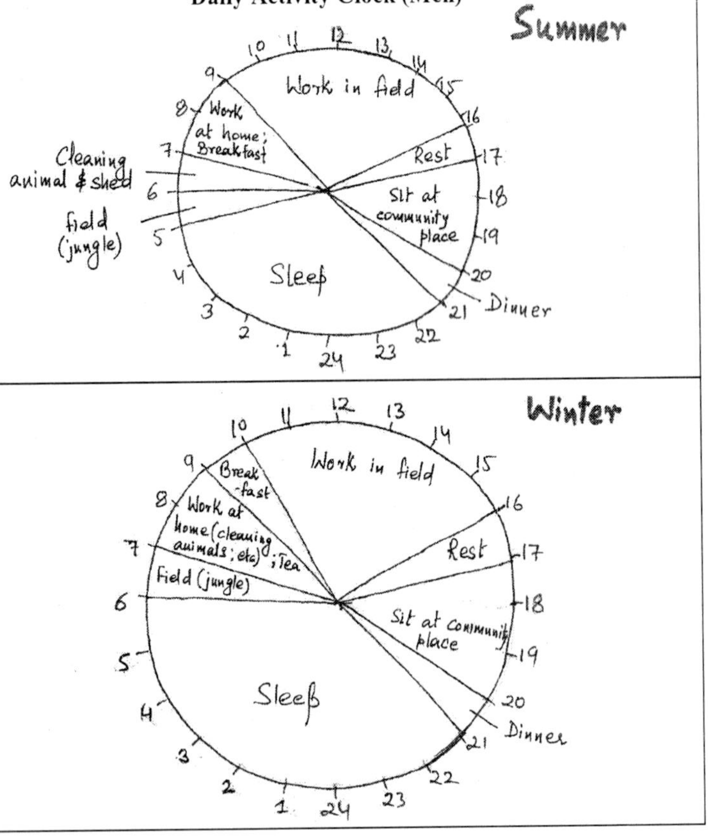

Daily Activity Clock (Women)

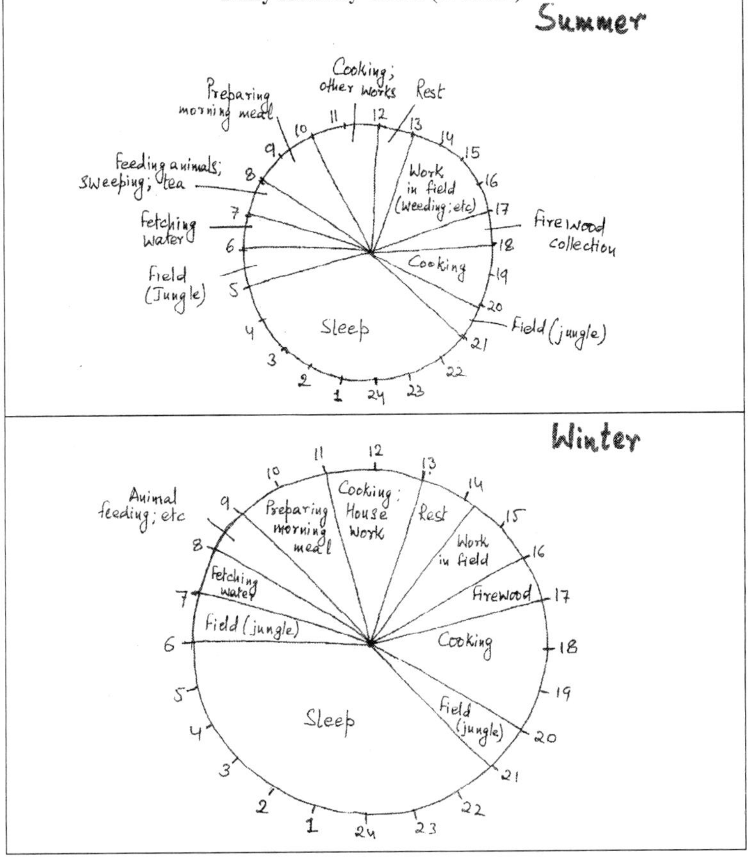

G. Mobility Map

Purpose

This tool is used to understand the mobility of males and females within and outside the community. It helps in learning the key places where people go, frequency, mode of transport and purpose. It also brings out the gender differences in mobility. It is useful in identifying and discussing issues related to access to water, land, community places, social meetings, etc. The differences and disparity in mobility can help while planning a program or project.

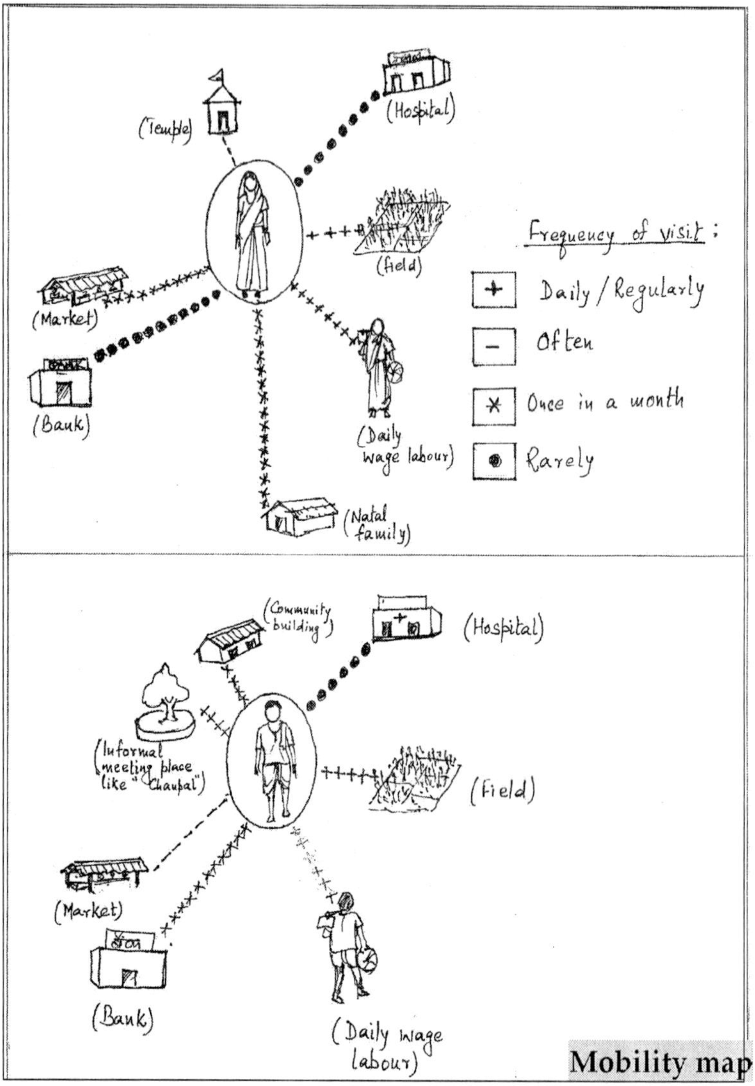

Mobility map

Process

Separate focus groups of males and females are organised. They are asked to enlist the key places they visit and categorise them as per frequency (daily, weekly, in a month or rarely). All the destination or places are represented by coloured, circular papers.

They are asked to put those places on the chart paper in order of relative distance from the respondents home.

Items

Chart paper, coloured papers, gum, sketch pens.

Caution

The relative distance of the places should be properly taken care of. Sometimes, the villagers have their own definition of distance, often expressed in terms of time taken; in such cases, facilitators need to convert the time taken into distance taking the terrain in mind. Mode, purpose and frequency must be noted on the chart. Places inside and outside the community must be clearly demarcated. Direction indicators must be followed.

Example

The following illustration shows the movement (including mode, purpose and frequency) of women to various places.

H. Venn Diagram

Purpose

It is a tool that is used to understand the role and importance of local groups and institutions. It helps in understanding the relationship, whether facilitating, conflicting or indifferent between participants and stakeholders (*i.e.* local organisations and groups). The size of circles symbolizes the importance attached to the body or organisation.

Process

A meeting of separate focus groups of males and females is organised. Circles of different coloured papers are prepared. They must be of different sizes too. The respondents are asked to list all the groups and organisations in the community as well as outside community, which are important. They are asked to represent each circle with an organisation. Then the circles are placed on a large chart paper depicting their inter-relationship as:

- Non-touching circles means no relationship or conflict;
- Touching borders of circles means no relationship but there is communication;
- Slight overlap means cooperation between agencies in responsibility handling and decision-making;
- Large overlap means lot of cooperation and almost "lock and key" relationship.

The participants can symbolize themselves with the largest circle and put themselves in the centre of the chart paper. Facilitate the respondents to think about agencies that are governmental, semi or non-governmental, or which are social, political, working on economic, environmental, health, education, gender or other issues. Facilitate the group in exploring how important and influential an agency is; whether they are satisfied with it.

Items

Chart paper, gum, different coloured papers, sketch pens and scissors.

Caution

The participants must be told not to assign agency's name to any circle or stick them, until consensus has been arrived. Facilitate the group to debate on their choice and decision.

The diagram prepared by one group should be compared with other group to ascertain the difference in opinion. The difference in opinion will be due to difference in relationship, so, it should be taken note of.

Example

The Venn-diagram represents the knowledge and opinion of males and females separately about the various agencies and organisations present inside and outside their community.

Stakeholder Venn diagram

I. Trend Line

Purpose

It is a tool which helps in understanding the change that has taken place in a community over a period of time. The change can be tracked through various angles and perspectives like change in cultivation pattern, traditional occupation, life style, eating habit, increase in population, health and disease, education, resources, social and physical infrastructure, quality of life, etc. It tells how the community perceives the changes, whether they think its improving or worsening or both.

Process

A meeting of separate focus groups of males and females is organised. It is necessary to involve the elderly in this exercise as they know more about the past and might bring out some hidden fact during the course of exercise. The respondents can be asked about changes taken place over the years vis-à-vis natural resources, population, infrastructure, girl education, etc.

A XY-axis graph is drawn where the horizontal axis depicts the year and the vertical axis depicts the increase or decrease of scale (high, medium, low) of a phenomenon. The extreme left of horizontal axis will represent the starting year and extreme right will represent current year. If the respondents are not clear about the years, they can be replaced by landmark events.

Trend lines

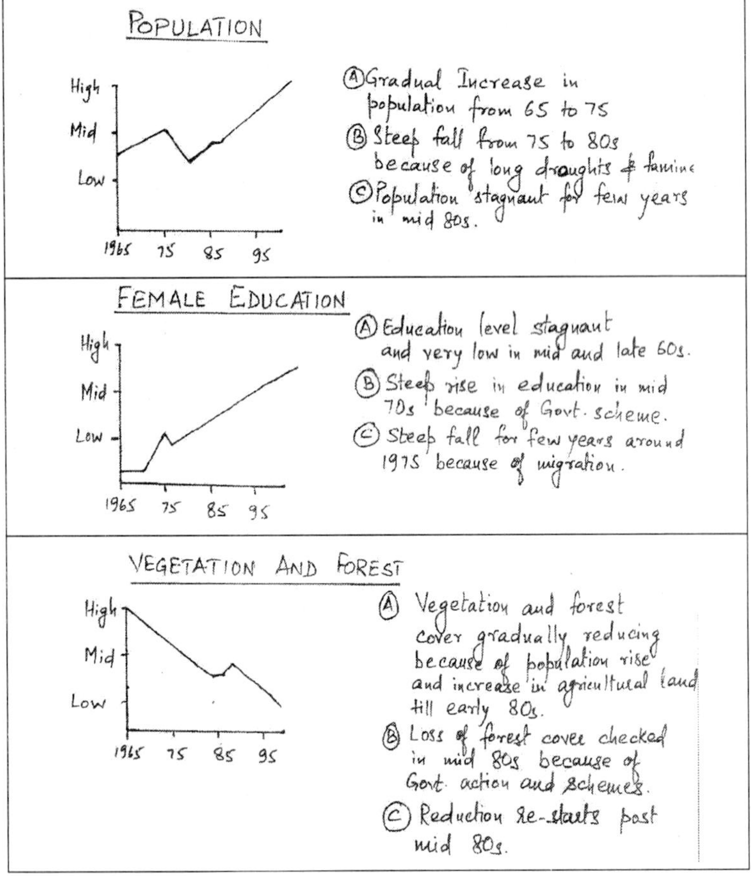

Simultaneously, the factors and reasons behind the trend are also discussed. One graph will represent the trend of one issue or phenomenon. All the trend line graphs are arranged one after another and discussed to check inter-relationship, linkage between issues. For example, migration may be directly or indirectly affecting the traditional occupation of the community.

Items

Chart paper, bold markers, sketch pens.

Caution

The reasons behind the trends should not be missed. Besides, past efforts and interventions should be recorded. Establish relation between similar looking issues. The participants can be asked to extend the trend line to future too.

Example

The graphs represent the trend lines of various phenomena.

J. Pair-Wise Ranking

Purpose

It is a tool that is used to gather information about the most pressing problem or priorities of the community. It helps to identify common as well as separate needs and aspirations of males and females and members of different socio-economic and age groups.

Process

Meeting of separate groups of key local informants based on socio-economic status and age is organised. They are asked to list their most important problems or needs.

The set of problems or needs are written on the vertical and horizontal axis of the pair-wise matrix. These problems are also written on separate small cards. The respondents are asked to choose the more important problem from a pair of problems. The choice is recorded on the matrix. The corresponding reason is also recorded separately. The process is repeated until all combinations are presented and decided. Now, the appearance of problems in the matrix is counted and ranked accordingly *i.e.* the problem which appears most is ranked highest.

It will be preferable if males and females respondents are taken together to conduct the exercise. Facilitating questions like why one problem is more pressing than the other are the problems inter-related? are problems of males different from females? which problems affect females more than males and vice-versa? can give the idea about how differently and similarly (gender-wise) problems are perceived.

PROBLEMS	Climate	Pests	Lack of Labour	Lack of Water	Lack of Expertise	Investment Cost	Soil Fertility
Climate	XXX	Climate	Climate	Climate	Climate	Climate	Climate
Pests	XXX	XXX	Pests	Pests	Pests	Pests	Soil Fertility
Lack of Labour	XXX	XXX	XXX	Lack of Water	Lack of Labour	Investment Cost	Soil Fertility
Lack of Water	XXX	XXX	XXX	XXX	Lack of Water	Investment Cost	Soil Fertility
Lack of Expertise	XXX	XXX	XXX	XXX	XXX	Investment Cost	Soil Fertility
Investment Cost	XXX	XXX	XXX	XXX	XXX	XXX	Soil Fertility
Soil Fertility	XXX	XXX	XXX	XXX	XXX	XXX	XXX

PROBLEMS	No. of Times Preferred	Rank
Climate	6	1
Pests	4	3
Lack of Labour	1	6
Lack of Water	2	5
Lack of Expertise	0	7
Investment Cost	3	4
Soil Fertility	5	2

Pair-wise ranking

Items

Blank pair-wise ranking matrix, markers and cards.

Caution

Respondents may get carried away to prepare a wish list, which has to be controlled and confined to developmental needs.

Example

The chart illustrates a list of problems and their ranking.

K. Problem Tree Chart

Purpose

This tool is used to further analyse the problems that have been identified by different groups. In this exercise, all the problems are discussed together with the community members to understand what the common and different perceptions of people are. It allows for a comprehensive discussion to look into the causes of a problem and the effects manifested. It clarifies to the participants themselves what they think about the cause-effect relationship that characterizes a problem.

Process

A meeting is organised where maximum participation of community members representing a mix of socio-economic background, males and females is ensured. The earlier identified problems are discussed individually in this exercise. The problem is written at the center of the chart. The causes are written beneath the problem and effects are written above it. The participants are facilitated to enlist as many cause and effects as they can. They are facilitated and asked to articulate and arrange the cause and effects as primary and subsidiary.

Problem tree chart

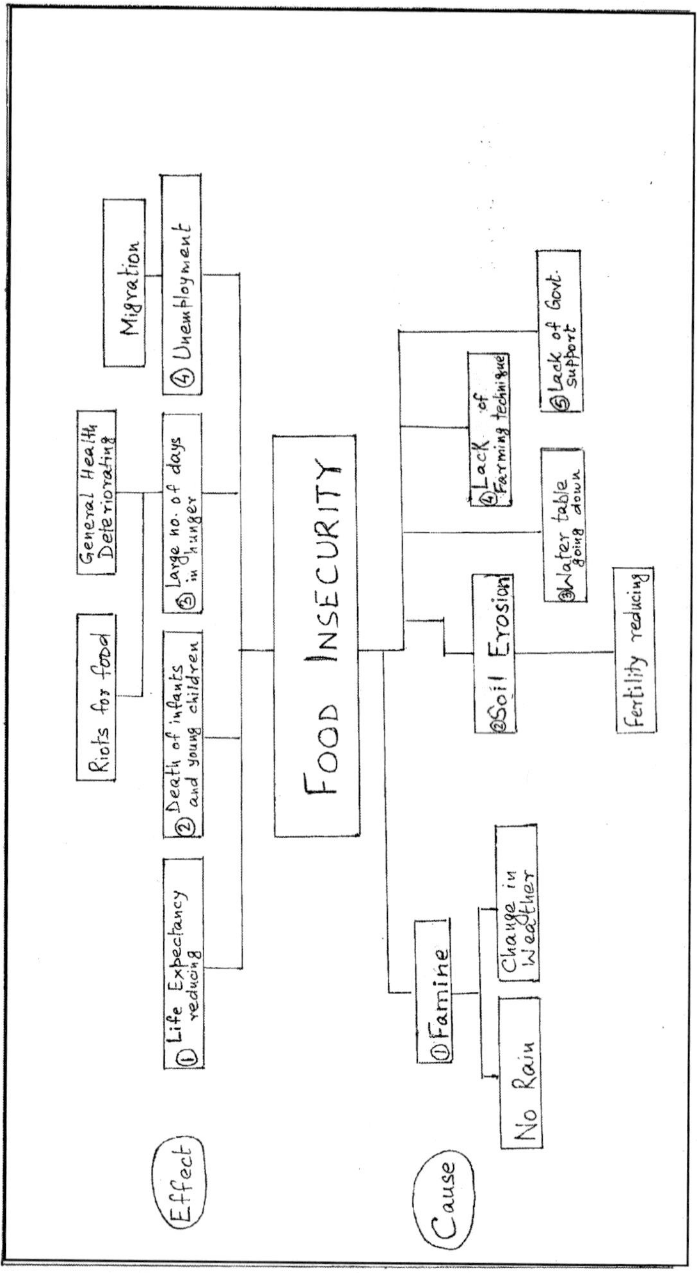

Items

Chart papers, sketch pens, bold markers

Caution

This is a brainstorming tool and lays the foundation for future plan of action. It is important to note that all the causes and effects should be related to the problem.

Example

The following chart shows the cause and effects of a community problem.

L. Problem Analysis Chart

Purpose

This tool is used to identify the existing mechanisms and explore possible strategies and opportunities while dealing with any problem or issue of the community. It is important to learn the existing coping mechanisms and survival strategies of the people as they can be used to develop future strategies. While conducting the exercise, external support from institutional stakeholders can be taken. There may arise a possibility of joint action plan through this exercise, where the traditional knowledge of the community and modern and technical knowledge of experts are combined.

Process

A meeting is organised where maximum participation of community members representing a mix of socio-economic background, and gender is ensured. Experts from external agencies may also be involved to make the exercise more beneficial. The findings of problem tree chart are discussed first. This will acquaint the externals about the local situation and perception as well as provide the community with a consolidated overview about what has been discussed in the problem tree exercise.

A table with four columns is prepared. The first column has the problem and its related issues. In case, more than one group has mentioned same problem, it should be mentioned once. The second column has the coping strategies *i.e.* the traditional practices and efforts taken up by the community. Here too, similarity must be shown by overlaps or simply marked. The third column has the opportunities or the technical suggestions given by the experts. The fourth column includes the consolidated solution taken from the ideas of community and experts.

Facilitating questions like which problems are shared by more than one group? what are the points of agreements and differences in prioritizing the problem or its solution? is the role of external support beneficial can bring out more feasible plan of action? should be asked.

Items

A copy of problem tree chart, pens, markers, chart papers.

Caution

Generally, this exercise may be conducted at the end of the process. It is therefore preferable that besides problem tree chart, other charts, maps and findings be also discussed before starting this exercise. It will be a sharing exercise with those community members who were not present in all of them.

List problems, strategies and opportunities with different colours. There may be few problems that cannot be handled. They should be mentioned nevertheless.

Example

The following chart shows the problem analysis chart of a community.

Problems	Coping strategies	Opportunities / suggestions	Consolidated solution
Food security	Reduction in number of meals. Eating kernels, seeds and wild berries. Migration.	Non-agricultural activity. Increase technical know-how. Ask for Government support.	Non-agricultural work. Apply for government subsidy or grant.
Health	Indigenous medicine and treatment. Faith healing or magic.	Medical facilities. Training. Vaccination.	Ask medical practitioners to arrange health camps. Training of first aid.
Sanitation	Open space.	Training and orientation. Construction of in-house toilet and seat.	Construction of cheap and subsidized seat and soak pit.
Water	Fetch water from distant places. Collect water in tanks and reservoirs.	Construction of tanks, check dams. Drip or Lift irrigation.	Seepage and percolation tanks. Taking up new irrigation methods. Digging wells.
Soil conservation	—	Plantation of trees. Check dams. Embankments.	Plantation of trees, shrubs and grass. Defining grazing area. Check dams.
Energy	Fuel and firewood	Bio-gas, cooking gas or kerosene.	Bio-gas.
Unemployment	Disguised unemployment. Migration.	Training and support for income generating activity.	Training and support for income generating activity.
Market	Small level business. Support of local moneylenders for credit needs. Barter system.	Formation of local groups and societies for credit needs. Information building about the market. Learning market skills.	Supply of goods to highest payer. Credit needs fulfilled through banks.

Problem analysis chart

Participatory Research

Research has been understood as a systematic and rigorous inquiry or investigation to enable people to understand social phenomena or events. There is usually a problem to be investigated, a process of inquiry followed and explanations offered to understand the nature of the problem. Discontent with the traditional research that tends to count, order and make decisions about human population, assuming the human beings have no 'agency'—as if they neither think nor act, has led to the development of a participatory research paradigm that includes participatory research, action research, community based action research, participatory action research etc. Opposition to the tyranny of the quantitative has led to a tradition of descriptive research methods, culminating in the ethno-methodological approach, which explores the meanings people construct and use in their everyday lives (See Beazley & Ennew, 2006). This approach takes an ideological position that insists on the involvement of the local people in the decision-making processes that affect their lives. The focus of participatory research is on generating knowledge from the perspective of those being researched, rather than from the perspective of the researcher. This helps identify and respond to local cultural, historical, socio-economic, geographical and political factors that influence the behaviour and practices of a community. People whose lives are being studied should be involved in defining the research questions and taking an active part in both collecting and analyzing data.

As Beazley & Ennew (2006), put it, PRA is based on the proposition that people construct social meanings and that every individual, regardless of education and status, is capable of research, analysis and planning. The practice of participatory research asserts that in practice, people should be active agents in their own lives; research should respect research participants' own words, ideas and understandings; researchers and research participants are equal; research methods should be flexible, exploratory and inventive; and both researchers and research participants should enjoy the research. With participatory behaviour and attitudes, the researchers role is to act as a facilitator, to establish trust, listen, learn and, as far as possible 'hand over the stick', or control to participants (Chambers, 1994). All people that would be affected by the research process are fully involved in the process to give everyone who has a stake, a voice and a choice.

By using participatory approaches, the researchers are able to gain access to people. A number of participatory methods and tools have been used in participatory research. The table gives an overview of the method, process and issues explored through the use of participatory approach.

Summary of the use of some participatory methods in Research

Method	*Issues explored*
Social Mapping	Importance of institutions in the community; where health services are, including tradition mid-wives; where children, single, pregnant women, old people live, etc.; where and how people spend their time; location and availability of transport
Resource Mapping	Where water pumps, wells, rivers are; wetland resources, where wood, fish, grass, thatch for roof is collected; location of gardens, crops, animals
Mobility Mapping	Mobility of men, women and children in rural and urban areas; where do they go to work, school, look for resources, for leisure, entertainment, for health seeking practices, to hang out/sleep (street children)
Body Mapping	To ascertain maternal health issues; issues of sexual abuse; where young people have been touched/abused; corporal punishment; where children have been hit
Social Network Diagrams	Questions asked of street children including who do you go to when you are lonely? When you are hungry? Scared? When you have a secret? When you need some money? When you are tired? When you have money and want to have fun, etc?
Matrix Ranking and Scoring	Severity and frequency of disease; types of food eaten in a community; health seeking preferences
Seasonal and Social Calendars	Wet, dry seasons; cycles of migration; cycles of religious events; work patterns; when people are rich; when poor; when people are sick
Time Transects	How people spend their time; time as a factor related to seeking services; time for being involved in work activities; time spent looking for food/resources
Causal Flow Analysis	Community perceptions of causes of infant and maternal mortality; reasons for going on the street (street children); reasons for migrating for work
Focus Group Discussions	Identification of community priorities; good for identifying questions for a interview schedule

Source: After Beazley & Ennew (2006)

Other Methods

There are certain communication skills which the researcher or field-worker should be equipped with while collecting data and seeking information of and from the community. These methods help in conducting the PRA or any other participative exercise.

Among the various methods, review of secondary data is non-participative but is necessary before any other method is applied. It provides the preliminary information and contextual background of the community and area. Besides, it is used for the purpose of triangulation and cross-checking. Direct observation is also non-participative and is used to see the community-building processes and the outcomes achieved. The observations made are later cross-checked through methods like individual and group interviews, meetings etc. These are direct communicating methods and carry their own significance and benefits. They can be used as per the requirement of the tool and the type of data/information needed.

Review of Secondary Data

It is an information-generation exercise done before entering the field and interacting with the community members. It provides necessary background information about the community, its inhabitants and their socio-political and economic set-up. It involves collection and review of existing literature, data, facts and information of the concerned area, target population and community as a whole. The sources of secondary data include project reports, annual reports, statistics, theses, dissertation, census reports, topographical maps (land or water based or environmental issue), aerial or satellite photos, etc. It helps to check the differences from the current data as well as cross-check information taken from primary sources. It provides a tentative base to design and plan field work.

Generally, secondary data and informations are first collected, identified and coded. Review of secondary data is useful to get an initial picture of the situation of the target group and socio-economic and institutional context as well as to determine gaps and possible contradictions in the available data. This helps to formulate alternative working hypothesis for the field study and to design the fieldwork. The data review is usually done by visiting libraries, government offices, universities, research centres, marketing bodies, etc.

Secondary information can be processed in two stages: First, the identification and compilation of the material, and then the analysis of the collected information. This is often initiated by grouping the information gathered according to the main themes of the study followed by the analysis and finally the formulation of the working hypotheses for the field study during which collected secondary data will be cross checked and gaps will be filled in.

Direct Observation

This is a first-hand data and information collecting technique. It is generally done without interacting much with the community. The information is gathered by noting down the things one sees happening at the time they happen, *e.g.* objects, conditions, events, processes, relationships among people, etc. In most cases, pre-set indicators and criterion are observed, for example, what do women do during day time? how do they interact within themselves and with men? what is the relationship of the poor in the community with the rich? how are separate informal groups interacting and behaving within and outside the community? who has access, control and ownership of vital resources of the community? etc.

The aim of observation is to document behaviour through watching and listening. Through observation it is possible to see what people are doing, when they do it, where they do it, and how they are doing it. We can use observation to gather information about the community-building process itself (*i.e.*, process evaluation) or the results it produced (*i.e.*, outcome evaluation).

The observations are made to see the trends and patterns. It can be used to cross-check data collected through focused group interviews and individual interviews.

Observations must be noted down at the same time or soon after observation has been completed, or else trivial-looking but critical points may be missed. The hypothesis arising from direct observation should be crosschecked with key informants or group interviews. Direct observation can also be used to check verbal information.

Direct observation is a useful tool to obtain intrinsic and otherwise hidden realities of the community. Observation can be either unstructured or structured in nature. In unstructured observation, observers generally do not look for specific things, nor do they record their observations in any particular manner.

Structured observation involves the systematic collection of specific pieces of information. Structured observation frequently involves the use of checklists, forms, or observation schedules on which observers record what they see. Observers receive training on how to recognize what they are looking for, as well as how to record what they observe. Sometime observers can record the presence of an actual behaviour or traces of behaviour.

Semi-Structured Interviews

Semi Structured Interviews (SSIs) are also called conversational interviews. They are interviews during which the interviewer limits the questions to a specific topic. It is partially structured by a flexible interview guide. This kind of guide ensures that the interview remains focused on the issue at hand while allowing enough conversation so that participants can introduce and discuss topics that are relevant to them. These tools are different from survey-type interviews which have lengthy, predetermined schedules.

Though normally the interviewer has a list of key questions, but he also follows the stream of issues brought up during the discussion. SSIs can be combined with any of the other PRA tools and are often complementary. Other PRA exercises describe a given situation, whereas the SSIs explain the reasons behind them. Where trendlines or seasonal calendars clarify changes over time, the SSIs can help to understand why these changes take place. Often SSIs are conducted with a specific group of people, who are in comparable situation and face similar problems.

SSIs are structured by using an advance list of key issues. They can be useful to obtain information in general or about a specific topic, to analyse problems and opportunities or to discuss plans as well as to elicit perceptions (*e.g.* on gender relations). It can be done by a team of 2-4 people of different backgrounds during or directly after PRA-exercises. It is advisable to spend not more than an hour on an individual interview and not more than two hours on a group interview.

Semi-structured interviews can be conducted at the individual level, the household level or the community level. To conduct semi-structured interviews, one should prepare an interview guide in advance. It should not be a conventional questionnaire but a list of issues and topics that have to be discussed. The sequencing of topics should be from simple to complex. Each topic should have set of initial questions (to introduce it to the respondents and prepare them to think over it) followed by probing and needling questions (to dig deeper, to get more details: what, why, who, when, how, how do you mean, anything else, but why, etc.). Preferably, one person should lead and control the direction and flow of the interview while another person can record the discussion.

One should deal with the topics one by one. Begin questioning by referring to something or someone visible. Ask your questions in an open-ended and probing way. Intersperse with probing questions and discussions; ask for concrete information, examples. Ask new (lines of) questions arising from the answers given. Allow the interviewed person also to raise her/his questions and discuss them. Involve other people in the discussion, if present. Pay attention to group dynamics.

It is important to include women as respondents, to encourage women to express themselves and to look for situations and places where women can express themselves freely. Depending on the purpose of the interview and the degree to which women can express themselves freely in the presence of men, group interviews may or may not be carried out with mixed groups. Interviews with small homogeneous groups of women can provide valuable information on their position in that society or on other sensitive issues.

Individual or Key Informant Interviews

A key informant is someone who, because of his or her unique position in a community, can provide us with important information about community-building. Some key informants have first-hand knowledge of the community and can provide us with their own assessment of what is happening. Others have access to information that would be difficult for us to obtain without their participation. In such cases, key informants pass along that information to us, often with an interpretation of what the data might mean to him. The use of key informants is a relatively simple and inexpensive means of collecting information. Key informants can be teachers, elected officials, youth, community leaders, agency staff, parents, and even funders.

Before interviewing key informants, one should know what type of information is needed from them. One approach is to write some key questions to cover each of the important topics, then a couple of potential follow-up questions for each key question. Ask factual questions about a particular topic first, then the opinion questions. Be sure to write open-ended rather than 'yes-no' questions. The goal is to be specific with questioning while allowing enough flexibility for open discussion.

Because of the nature of the information key informants provide, it is often difficult to ensure their anonymity. In many cases, the key informant is the only person who could have provided a particular piece of information. We should make sure that the key informant is comfortable with the way we plan to use the information we collect. Maintain a neutral attitude throughout the interview. Don't argue with the key informant's assessment of a situation. Be prepared to probe or use follow-up questions to gather additional information that might clarify why the key informant sees the situation as he or she does.

Household Interviews

These are interviews with specially selected households. When interviewing households, one will interview adult male and female members of the household separately, followed by a discussion on certain issues with the whole household. Sometimes it is also interesting to interview older and younger women separately since this might indicate ongoing changes in the position of women. If possible, let a male member of the team interview the male members of the household and the female team member the females in the household. Households may be selected from each of the socio-economic categories in the population or any other agreed criteria.

Focus Group Meetings

Focus group meeting is a compromise between participant-observation, which is less controlled, lengthier, and more in-depth, and preset interviews, which are not likely to attend to participants' own concerns. It is relatively low-cost, semi-structured, small group (four to twelve participants plus a facilitator) consultation used to explore peoples' attitudes, feelings, or preferences, and to build consensus.

The goal of any focus group is to promote self-disclosure among participants. Because a group, rather than an individual, is asked to respond to questions, there is possibility of dialogue. Participants take lead from the comments of others and add a richness to the dialogue that could not be achieved through a one-on-one interview.

Members of a focus group should have some characteristics in common. For example, the information we need to collect might suggest that we need to conduct a focus group composed of middle-school girls. Even though participants in a focus group are similar in one or two desired characteristics, the group must also include enough diversity in other characteristics to provide an accurate portrayal of the group's collective opinion. For example, the group might be composed of middle-school girls who represent the racial, ethnic and economic diversity of the middle school's population.

An important step in preparing for the focus group interview is the development of a set of questions that encourage participants to respond. Good questions sound conversational and natural. They are usually short, open-ended, and one-dimensional (*i.e.,* they ask for only one piece of information at a time). Begin with an introductory question that will get people talking and make them feel comfortable. Gradually move into the topic you want them to discuss with a transition question that is followed by several key questions covering the major areas of interest. The specific order in which the questions are asked is called the questioning route. A good questioning route has an easy beginning, flows logically and naturally from one question to another, and moves from the general to the specific. It is important to estimate the time required to exhaust the discussion on each question. These time estimates can be used to help manage the interviews.

Moderation of group discussion is one of its integral component and requirement. Effective moderating requires preparation, mental discipline, and skill in facilitating group interaction. Importantly, moderators must believe that all participants have something to contribute to the discussion regardless of their education level, experience, or background. Moderators must listen attentively, with sensitivity, and try to understand the perspective of each participant. Lack of respect is quickly transmitted to participants and results in reduced and often distorted contributions.

Role Playing

Enables people to creatively remove themselves from their usual roles and perspectives to allow them to understand choices and decisions made by other people. Ranging from a simple story with only a few characters to an elaborate street theater production, this tool can be used to accelimatise a PRA team to a project setting, train trainers, and encourage community discussions about a particular development intervention.

5

Participatory Monitoring and Evaluation

Monitoring and Evaluation (M&E) are increasingly being recognized as indispensable tools of project management. M&E provides a basis for accountability in the use of development resources. Given the greater transparency now expected of the development community, government and agencies assisting them need to respond to calls for more 'success on the ground' with examples of development impact and with evidence that they have systems in place that support earning from experience.

Participatory monitoring and evaluation (PM&E) has emerged because of recognition of the limitations of the conventional approach. It is attracting interest from many quarters since it offers new ways of assessing and learning from change that are more inclusive, and more in tune with the views and aspirations of those most directly affected.

PM&E provides an opportunity for development organisations to focus better on their ultimate goal of improving the lives of poor people. By broadening involvement in identifying and analysing change, a clearer picture can be gained of what is really happening on the ground. It allows people to celebrate successes, and learn from failures. For those involved, it can also be a very empowering process, since it puts them in charge; helps develop skills, and shows that their views count.

There are many different forms of PM&E depending on who is participating, at what stages they are involved, and the precise objectives. At the heart of PM&E, however, are four broad principles:

- '**Participation**'—which means opening up the design of the process to include those most directly affected, and agreeing to analyse data together;
- The inclusiveness of PM&E requires '**negotiation**' to reach agreement about what will be monitored or evaluated, how and when data will be collected and analysed, what the data actually means, and how findings will be shared, and action taken;
- This leads to '**learning**' which becomes the basis for subsequent improvement and corrective action;
- Since the number, role, and skills of stakeholders, the external environment, and other factors change over time, '**flexibility**' is essential (IDS, 1998).

PME 'flips' the traditional 'top-down' development approach to a 'bottom-up' approach, which encourages, supports and strengthens communities' existing abilities to identify their own needs, set their own objectives, and monitor and evaluate them.

Monitoring is defined as the 'continuous internal assessment of project implementation in relation to agreed schedules and of the use of inputs, infrastructure, and services by project beneficiaries'. On the other hand, evaluation has been defined as 'an internal or external management activity to assess whether a program is achieving its intended objectives'. An M&E system answers questions of relevance (does the project address our needs?), efficiency (are we using resources wisely?), effectiveness (are the desired results achieved?), and impact (to what extent have project activities brought about changes for the betterment of individuals and/or community?).

Monitoring helps in ensuring that the programme achieves its defined objectives within its prescribed time frame and financial allocations. Monitoring provides regular feedback on progress of programme implementation, and the problems faced. It helps in tracking resource acquisition and allocation, costs, production and delivery of services as also the degree and quality of stakeholder participation. Monitoring can be conducted at different levels like the policy, programme and project. An example is given in the following table.

Table: Levels of Monitoring

	Infant health	*Girls education*
Policy Monitoring	Decreasing infant mortality rates	Increasing girls education attainment
Program Monitoring	Information on pre-natal care targeted to pregnant women	Expanding capability of school facilities
Project Monitoring	Awareness of good pre-natal care in 6 targeted villages	Number of girls completing primary education

Monitoring is a type of surveillance system to see that every thing goes as nearly as possible, as per plan and that resources are not wasted. Participatory monitoring involves the beneficiaries of a project in measuring, recording, collecting, processing and communicating information to assist the project management and group members in decision making. 'Monitoring is a continuous feedback system, on-going throughout the life cycle of a project or programme, and involves the overseeing or periodic review of each activity, at every level of implementation to ensure that:

(a) Inputs are ready on time;
(b) Work plans are followed as closely as possible;
(c) Adjustments can be made, and corrective action taken where necessary;
(d) People who need to know are kept informed;
(e) Constraints and bottlenecks can be foreseen, & timely solutions found; and
(f) Resources are used efficiently and effectively.

Evaluation is the application of systematic methods to assess the programme/project/policy for:

- The appropriateness of programme design and implementation methods in achieving specified objectives and broader developmental objectives;
- The programme results, both intended and unintended;
- Factors affecting the level and distribution of benefits produced;
- The projects sustainability; and
- Attribution of causality: Can the observed changes be attributed to the project and not other factors?

Some of the questions to be asked as part of the evaluation could be whether participation in the micro-credit programme increases the household income of the participants? What else might have affected household income? Did the micro-credit programme reduce poverty in the community? and what else might have affected poverty in the community?

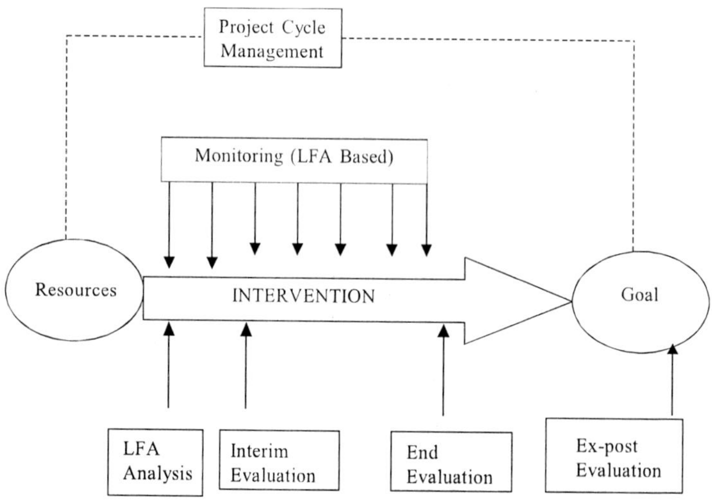

Source: COWI, 2000

Fig: Monitoring and Evaluation in the Project Cycle Management

Baseline data

The first step in the design of the M&E for a programme or project is the baseline survey. The baseline survey is designed to:

- Establish a bench mark which would help in measuring the subsequent change;
- Provide information on the situation in the project area and target groups in relation to project development goals, for project planning and process monitoring
- Measure the project benefits; and
- To guide and inform facilitators.

A baseline study reveals the situation in the project area before the intervention. The resulting benchmark data is used for comparison when using indicators though the project cycle. Baseline data against which the progress and results can be measured needs to be disaggregated by sex, socio-economic and ethnic grouping, and age. If we want to answer whether a programme made a difference, we should be able to show that our key measures changed in the way we hoped. Before and after measures enable us to measure change. By comparing key measures after the programme against the same measures taken before the programme began, we are able to measure change. The before measure is called the baseline. The baseline would be useful while implementing a quasi-experimental evaluation design. This would also necessitate a control group along with the project baseline sample.

The baseline survey can either be carried out, on a sample basis, or on a census basis, in the project villages and localities prior to the interventions. The baseline can be prepared by canvassing a village schedule or through participatory tools like resource and social mapping, wealth ranking etc. Information on aspects like those given below may be obtained:

- Literacy;
- Health, ailments, infant mortality;

- Access to minimum needs like fuel, source, access to drinking water, and presence of sanitary facilities;
- Drudgery causing activities to women;
- Food security and nutrition including frequency of consumption of food items, management of shortage of food;
- Time-use profile for both men and women;
- Skill base;
- Household expenditure, savings and borrowings pattern; and
- Migration; etc.

The baseline data gives a representative profile of the situation in the project area. As the data is based on a sample, only broad generalizations can be attempted. It is important that before actual planning for interventions, a detailed reality check based on participatory approaches is attempted. The baseline survey provides a listing of issues and problems concerning the area and the target group. It helps in identifying the most prevalent problems and issues. The baseline also provides an idea of the magnitude of the problem. It tells us as to on an average, what proportion of the households is affected by a particular problem?

The baseline also helps in prioritizing which issues and problems are more pressing than the other and which need immediate attention of the project. One of the simple ways of prioritizing problems is to find out what proportions of persons are affected by the problem? The problems can then be ranked depending on number of persons being affected by the same (See pair-wise ranking, Ch. 4). However, sometimes, a large number of people may suffer from a problem, but there may be some other pressing problem, which numerically speaking may be lesser in magnitude but high in depth and intensity. It is the responsibility of the user to facilitate the community to prioritise the problems. The baseline can help in sensitizing the district and block administration of the problems and issues in the area. This data can be shared with the district and block administration as well as with the bankers, line departments and other agencies. It can also be shared with local level press and significant persons so as to create awareness about the problems and issues of the area.

Facilitator can use the data available from the baseline as a starting point for situational analysis of the area. Such a situational analysis is to be attempted with the help of the local community. PRA based methods need to be used for the purpose. This serves another purpose, *i.e.* it helps the community reflect on its own situation when a larger picture is presented before them. This may spur them on to some concrete actions. A comparative picture of the situation in other areas can also be used, which might help in the reflection process. The process of reflection may initiate introspection within the community and they may enter into an analysis of the causes of the situation they are in as also identify who is responsible for the particular situation. Action points with specific responsibilities of the different actors can then be delineated. As sometimes development workers tend to think on predictable lines, a process of innovation can also be triggered when the community is involved in the problem reflection.

It is the responsibility of the user to cross check the data if there is reason to believe that the accuracy of information is inadequate. Some of the reasons for inadequacy may be that inappropriate data may be collected through weaknesses in classification (small landholding migrants classified as landless), breakdowns in data collection or recording etc. In addition, sometimes, information may be technically correct but not an adequate description of the situation.

This cross checking can be done by spot-checks. Spot checks provide valuable information to correct false impressions created by faulty data. While conducting spot checks it is important to plan. The user should first decide how many places to visit and where. She should keep in mind the need to select locations that adequately represent the nature of the information problem that is being addressed. It is also necessary to decide before hand whom to talk to-officials, non-officials or a mix etc.

Data can be a good servant as well as a bad master if not used properly. There is a need to be extremely sensitive to the data and the situation it represents. We have to recognize that beneath the ratios and percentages, lays a lot of diversity. We have to learn to recognize the diversity. Also, once converted into ratios and proportions, the human being tends to be forgotten. We should not lose sight of the person. The data generated by the baseline needs to be supplemented by other sources also. We may have to refer to the Census, SRS or other research studies conducted by other departments, academics and NGOs. Also, in order to add a qualitative dimension to the issues, PRA based methods have to be used.

A **participatory baseline** provides a description and information, mainly from the insiders' perspective, of a specific situation. It is done so that activities can be focused, and change can be measured by comparison with similar situations at some future time. Information is identified and collected to describe the present situation as it specifically relates to the objectives. For example, if one of the objectives is to increase the supply of fuelwood to a community, the baseline information required might include:

What is the present fuelwood supply?

What is the source of the present fuelwood supply (local and/ or imported)?

What is household fuelwood consumption?

The main purpose is to establish criteria to measure change. A participatory baseline enables insiders to measure and evaluate change in specific conditions providing a common understanding, from the beginning, of how change will be measured. Participatory baselines have several advantages. Firstly, with the use of participatory baselines, community can readily observe change and discuss and agree upon ways to measure and observe change. Participatory baseline provides a way to obtain information when needed, that is when insiders need specific information about an activity or proposed activity, the baseline method is a way for them to organize and obtain the information. Baseline surveys by facilitators are often costly, and unintelligible to the local community. Participatory baselines complement and enrich outsider baselines by providing a comparison of the perceptions of insiders and facilitators. As both local community and the facilitators are involved in the process of planning and analysis of baselines, it is a learning experience for both groups. The information is understandable and can be used for corroboration of problem identification and solutions, planning project activities and identifying potential problems.

Participatory baselines can be done with the whole community or with the small beneficiary group. This will depend on the size of the community and their interest. If there is a large community group, it may be best if responsibilities for baseline are delegated to a few people (a baseline team). The baseline team may go by the baseline issues developed by the larger group and report the results back to them. Facilitators generally have access to information from urban markets, libraries, other agencies and government sources which can be useful to local communities.

Participatory monitoring is the systematic recording and periodic analysis of information that has been chosen and recorded by insiders with the help of facilitators. One of the main purposes of participatory monitoring is that it provides information during the life of the project, so that adjustments and/or modifications/ mid-course corrections can be made if necessary. Participatory monitoring is not only about recording. It is also stopping at predetermined stages in the project to analyze information generated by the monitoring process. The stages at which monitoring information is to be analysed are generally predetermined and would vary according to the nature of the project and its activities as well as the local context of the community.

However, before participatory monitoring begins, the community must understand why they are monitoring. Information should keep everyone informed of progress (or lack of progress) toward planned objectives and activities. When the terms of measurement, are chosen by insiders, the information is better understood. It is always advisable to go by the local terms of measurement that is seasons instead of months, bags and sacks instead of kilograms and tones. The chances of monitoring continuing in the future are more likely. Additionally, if this kind of information is required by facilitators, they can translate the insiders' terms of measurement into terms that they use. It is important to recognise that local communities have the capacity and ability to creatively analyse both kinds of information, descriptive as well as quantitative for a complete analysis.

One important benefit of participatory monitoring is that it provides an ongoing picture that allows the community to determine whether activities are progressing as planned. It may also show when activities are not leading to objectives, so that early adjustments can be made. Also, data generated by the process of participatory monitoring acts as an early warning system, that helps identify problems at an early stage. Solutions can then be sought before the problems get out of hand. Continuous feedback throughout the life of the activities ensures that the quality of the activities is sufficient to provide good and sustainable results. It also helps to have an optimal allocation of resources for better results. Additionally, it is interesting that when the local community is involved they are able to locate the data relative to their past experience. This lends a unique quality to the information, something that is not possible in monitoring conducted by facilitators. Information provided by participatory monitoring also influences the direction of future evaluation; it becomes more realistic and grounded.

One of the issues involved in participatory projects is monitoring the participation of the people. Both insiders and facilitators can monitor participation, but it may be for very different reasons. Facilitators may be interested in equal community representation in decision making, while insiders may be interested in equal distribution of costs and benefits. Participation is often an outsider objective because they are concerned with equal representation of all elements and groups in the community. Facilitators may want to ensure, through monitoring participation, that all involved and affected people in the community are represented when decisions regarding activities are made. Because "participation" is a process that emerges and develops as the activities progress information needs regarding participation may undergo significant change over time.

Local communities may also monitor their own participation depending on how they look at participation. They may wish to know who participates in communal activities, so that benefits can be equitably distributed. An ideal mix would be when both the facilitators as well as the local community get together to monitor. It makes sense to have insiders define it and help either measure it or help facilitators identify indicators. When insiders choose participation indicators, they are likely to be more locally relevant than indicators chosen by facilitators.

While developing the monitoring and evaluation systems in projects, it is worthwhile to follow the model approach. A model is a simplified abstraction of the programme or project. It represents the major parts or elements, of the programme and their relationships. The models also help us visualize a programme in context. It helps to think analytically about cause and effect and identifies key assumptions that can be tested. Using models also helps understand causality, did the programme cause a change? are the changes we observe a consequence of the programme? What else besides the programme contributed to the observed changes? etc.

Input indicators monitor project-specific resources to be provided for each project item; usually used at or close to the start of the project whereas output indicators measure output for each project or component, such as improvements in relation to baseline test data. They determine whether project goals are being achieved and they are used near to the end of the funder's involvement. Outcome indicators measure the immediate impacts produced by each of the outputs. On the other hand, impact indicators measure the medium and long-term impacts of the project. They are usually used after the funder's involvement is complete. Risk/enabling indicators measure the influence of external factors on the project. The butterfly model of planning and evaluation (Fig 19) depicts how planning can break down goals into more specific ones and define concrete outputs to meet these goals, which can in turn be evaluated to determine whether or not they have met the specific and broad goals (Karl, 1999).

Fig. 19: Blankenberg's Butterfly Model of Planning and Evaluation

Long Term Goal (impact)	Medium term Objective (Effects)	Short Term Objectives (Outputs)	Planned Activities	Implemented Activities	Achieved Outputs	Achieved Effects	Achieved Impacts
Empowerment of Women	Increased Knowledge of Women	Publication of bulletin on Women's Rights	Information Gathering Editing Articles Producing Newsletter	Information Collected Articles Edited Newsletter Prepared	Newsletter Publication	Women's Knowledge of their Rights Increased	Contribution To Empowerment of Women
planning				monitoring	Evaluation of Output	Evaluation of Effects	Evaluation of Impacts

Source: Blankenberg F. (1994)

A participatory self-monitoring system developed by the NABARD for the Maharashtra Rural Credit Programme (NABARD, undated) is a very good model of a participatory system for women. In this tool, two sets of parameters, one for the monthly monitoring and the other for annual monitoring, have been developed. These parameters are represented visually through simple line sketches that make it easy to identify as to what the pictures represent. After participatory self-assessments in group meetings, members are required to rank the group on each parameter into three categories, viz, good, average or bad, indicated by green, yellow and red colours.

Table: Parameters for Participatory Self-Monitoring

Parameters	*Good [green]*	*Average [yellow]*	*Bad [red]*
	MONTHLY SELF MONITORING PARAMETERS		
Preparation for meeting	All necessary arrangements for meeting are made	More than half the arrangements for the meeting are made	No preparations at all for the meeting
Holding meetings regularly	Meetings held as per predetermined dates	Meetings held on day other than predetermined dates	No meeting was held
Meetings on scheduled time	Meeting starts on scheduled time	Meeting starts late	Meeting starts late by more than two hours
Attendance in meeting	All members attend the meeting	More than 75% attendance	Less than 75% attendance
Proceedings (minutes) of the meeting	Proceedings are recorded and read in the next meeting	Proceedings are recorded but not read in the next meeting	Proceedings are not recorded
Savings	All members deposit their saving on a fixed date	More than 90% members deposit their saving on a fixed date	Less than 90% members deposit their saving on a fixed date
Account keeping	Recording of all accounts completed in the meeting itself	Accounts are completed after the meeting	Accounts are incomplete or not kept at all

(contd.)

(contd.)

Parameters	*Good [green]*	*Average [yellow]*	*Bad [red]*
Collective decision making	Collective decisions are taken	Only few members participate in discussion and decision making	Decisions are taken without discussion
Repayment	All members repay loan in time	95% repayment in time	Less than 95% repayment in time
Lending	Loan disbursements upto 95% of available resources	Loan disbursements less than 95% of available resources	No loan disbursement at all
Petty cash	No cash is kept more than the limit fixed	More cash kept than limit fixed	Entire amount of saving is kept in cash
Insurance	Insurance of members and assets acquired by them through group loan and its renewal	Insurance of some members and assets	No insurance
Community activities-discussion and action	Community development activities are discussed and undertaken	Community development activities are discussed	No discussion and no action on community development
ANNUAL SELF MONITORING PARAMETERS			
Sharing of responsibilities	More than 50% of members share the responsibilities	Upto 50% members share the responsibilities	No sharing of responsibilities
Common fund	Common fund is created	No common fund	—
Lending	More than 60% members' loan needs met	Loan needs of 30 to 60% members met	Less than 30% members' loan needs met
Income generation	More than 50% increase in income in case of members who have taken loan	25 to 50% increase in income in case of members who have taken loan	Less than 25% increase in income in case of members who have taken loan

(contd.)

(contd.)

Parameters	*Good [green]*	*Average [yellow]*	*Bad [red]*
Outside financial assistance	Outside financial assistance taken	No outside financial assistance taken	—
Insurance	Insurance of members and assets acquired by them through group loan and its renewal	Insurance of some members and assets	—
Training	As decided by group 4 or more training programmes in a year	As decided by group 2 to 3 or more training programmes in a year	No training
Inter group lending	Inter-group lending resorted	No inter-group lending is resorted	—
Audit	Accounts of group audited	—	Accounts of group not audited
Formation of new groups	Help is extended for formation of new groups	No help is extended for formation of new groups	—
Appointment of record keeper	—	Record keeper appointed	Record keeper is not appointed
Repayment	100% repayment as scheduled	95 to 99% repayment as scheduled	Less than 95% repayment
Formation of clusters	Participation in cluster	No participation in cluster	—
Representation on local bodies	Members of group on elected local bodies	No members of group on elected local bodies	—
Community development	4 or more community development programmes undertaken	1 to 3 community development programmes undertaken	No community development programmes undertaken
Annual meeting	Annual meeting is held	No annual meeting is held	—

Participatory Evaluation: provides for the active involvement in the evaluation process of those with a stake in the programme; providers, partners, customers (beneficiaries) and other interested parties, and it takes place throughout all phases of evaluation: planning and design, gathering and analyzing data; identifying the evaluation findings; preparing conclusions and recommendations; disseminating results; and preparing an action plan to improve programme performance (IFAD, ANGOC & IIRR, 2001). These evaluations are oriented to the information needs of programme stakeholders rather than the funder and can include some or the full arrays of stakeholders. All stakeholders get to communicate and negotiate, to reach a consensus on evaluation findings, to solve problems and to make plans for improving the performance. During these interactions, the views of all participants are sought and recognized, allowing for participation by less strong stakeholders. The focus of the participatory evaluation is on identification of lessons learned which would help in improving programme implementation. It is recognized that enhanced participation, especially of beneficiaries, in monitoring and evaluation helps improve understanding of the development process itself.

Differences between conventional and participatory evaluation

	Conventional	*Participatory*
WHO	External experts	Community members, project staff, facilitator
WHAT	Predetermined indicators of success, principally cost and production outputs	People identify their own indicators of success, which may include production outputs
HOW	Focus on 'scientific objectivity'; distancing of evaluators from other participants, uniform, complex procedures; delayed, limited access to results	Self evaluation; simple methods adopted to local culture; open, immediate sharing of results through local involvement in evaluation processes
WHEN	Usually upon completion of project/programme; sometimes also mid-term	More frequent; small scale evaluations
WHY	Accountability, usually summative, to determine if funding continues	To empower local people to initiate, control and take corrective action

Source: Narayan-Parker, 1993 quoted in IFAD, ANGOC and IIRR (2001).

The technique of participatory M&E has an edge over other conventional M&E systems, in the sense that it examines the relevant issues with the involvement of al concerned. It also helps in promoting better understanding of the others' point of view by offering stakeholders the opportunity to communicate their concerns. Participatory evaluation enables the community to measure its own progress and improves its evaluation skills. One of the important benefits of participatory evaluation is that it increases the likelihood that the evaluation information would be acted upon. By using teamwork in the process, a shared commitment to act on evaluation recommendations is built up.

It is important that while using participatory evaluation, the stakeholders are conscious of the fact that the evaluation may be viewed as less objective, since it involves all stakeholders with possible vested interests. This is a real danger; some stakeholders may use the opportunity to manipulate the process to further their own interests.

Participatory evaluation provides an opportunity for both facilitators and the local community to stop and reflect on the past in order to make decisions about the future. Insiders are encouraged and supported by facilitators to take responsibility and control of:

- planning what is to be evaluated
- how the evaluation will be done
- carrying out the evaluation
- analyzing information and presenting evaluation results.

It makes sense for facilitators to help insiders conduct an effective evaluation. With the results of evaluation, insiders may choose to continue activities, modify all or some, change the strategy, change the objectives, or discontinue activities. Facilitators may assist the local community in planning and conducting the evaluation. They may lead but not direct. They can provide the focus, the idea, and some help, intervening when assistance is required.

Participatory evaluations are not conducted for the purpose of answering the questions that facilitators need answered.

However, in many instances, insider and facilitator evaluation questions may be the same and both may be answered through participatory evaluation.

Participatory evaluation provides information to guide management decisions. A participatory evaluation is not a final judgment on whether activities are successful or unsuccessful. The information should encourage changes and adjustments either during the life span of the activities, for future phases of the activities, or for future new activities.

In a participatory evaluation, people learn more about the things that have worked well, and why they worked. They also learn more about the things that haven't worked well, and why they didn't. When the people involved go through the process of examining, it is more likely that corrective measures will be implemented in the future because they are discovered and understood by the community.

In a participatory evaluation, the overall and immediate objectives, their continued relevance, and the effectiveness of the activities are all taken into account. Participatory evaluation is done in light of original objectives and uses much of the information from Participatory Assessments, Participatory Baselines, and Participatory Monitoring can be used in participatory evaluation. Participatory evaluations help in better decision making by the local community, and by examining the activities individually and relative to objectives, give insiders relevant and useful information. Helping them decide whether the objectives and/or activities should stay the same or change.

Participatory evaluation reveals hidden and undervalued community skills, and/or develops analytical skills needed to make good decisions. It helps the local community better organize and express their concerns and interests in ways facilitators can understand. This strengthens two way communication. The process of participatory evaluation also helps the outsides have a better understanding of the local community. The facilitators benefit from this process as it complements and enriches their own evaluations. This is especially so when the facilitators objectives are self-help and sustainability. A participatory evaluation will let them know whether or not the community is likely to continue the activities when facilitators have left.

As with participatory monitoring, participatory evaluation also strengthens local community to facilitator communication. Information from participatory evaluations can be used by insiders and facilitators to identify strong and weak points of activities. If activities are to be continued, or phased over to insiders, information can be used to modify activities and make them more effectively meet objectives, and better respond to real community needs and priorities.

'Evaluations' are increasingly being replaced with 'impact assessment'. Impact assessment gives greater focus on the outcomes of the interventions, rather than inputs and outputs. While the goals of impact assessment studies commonly incorporate both 'proving' impacts and 'improving' interventions, impact assessments are more likely to prioritise the proving goal than did the evaluations of the 1980s (David H., 1998).

"In the most generic sense, impact analysis is any process which seeks to determine if an intervention has had the desired outcome. If the intervention is, for example, an immunization programme, and the desired outcome is to prevent polio, the impact analysis would focus on polio rates. If it could be shown that polio rates went down, as a result of the immunizations, the programme's impact could be deemed successful. In other words the impact analysed should correspond to the sought—after outcome (Ledgerwood, 1998)".

Impacts can occur at several levels, the individual, group, household and other broader levels. It can also occur in the economic, socio/political/cultural and personal/psychological categories. In the economic sphere, impact may be in terms of business expansion or transformation of enterprises, accumulation of wealth at the level of the community or household or in terms of income or economic resource protection or reducing the vulnerability of the poor. Impacts in the socio/political/cultural spheres may be related to changes in power and status relationships, redistribution of assets, power or decision-making or changes in children's nutrition or education etc. A number of impacts can also be discerned at the personal/psychological level. Women achieve more power in the household or community as the result of access to financial services. They may start feeling more confident of themselves, acquire the ability to face outsiders more confidently, start taking small risks in enterprises etc. In short, the quality of life of the women would undergo a positive change after their coming together.

Engendering Participatory Monitoring and Evaluation

As discussed earlier, participatory monitoring and evaluation makes it possible to identify problems in the early stages of the project, and gives communities and implementing agencies the ability and flexibility to respond to changing scenario that may affect the project interventions. It taps the perspectives and insights of all stakeholders, beneficiaries as well as project implementers. All stakeholders identify issues, analyse findings and make recommendations as well as take responsibility for necessary action. Stakeholders who are involved in the identification of problems and solutions will develop ownership and commitment to any corrective measures adopted.

The first steps for integrating gender concerns into the participation process include:

- Identifying the key stakeholders and ensuring that they will all be invited to participate during consultations.
- Assessing the current scope, level and quality of participation.
- Identifying and setting measures to strengthen the capacity of weak and vulnerable groups, including women, to participate.

It needs to be seen whether participatory processes are being encouraged among stakeholders, both men and women, when:

- Setting goals
- Setting targets
- Identifying activities and indicators
- Planning, implementing, and maintaining projects
- Selecting the best data collection methods
- Collecting and analyzing data
- Monitoring and evaluating
- Reporting and disseminating results

Gender sensitive monitoring and evaluation reveals the extent to which a project has addressed the different needs of men and women, and has made an impact on their lives and overall social and economic well-being. It also improves project performance during implementation and allows for mid-term corrections, and makes it possible to derive lessons for future projects. An effective gender-sensitive monitoring and evaluation system requires that key activities be undertaken at different points in the project cycle.

Project Identification and Preparation

- Engender benchmark survey design/baseline study,
- Undertake an initial gender study to broadly cover social, cultural and economic aspects: identify potential negative impacts of project interventions on women as well as men,
- Ensure PRA addresses gender related issues,
- Conduct a detailed gender analysis and social assessment,
- Identify gender related goals and priorities based on available information and consultation with stakeholders,
- Assess institutional capacity for gender integration into development activities.

Design and Appraisal

- Ensure gender is integrated into goals and objectives and set clear targets,
- Plan for developing capacity to address gender issues and to monitor and evaluate progress,

- Set up a monitoring and evaluation system,
- Engender the Logical Framework,
- Identify and select key gender sensitive indicators for input, output, outcome and impact,
- Develop/Select the 'best' data collection method and decide on timing,
- Organise reporting and feedback processes, clearly identifying who will collect and analyse information and when, and who will receive it.

Implementation

- Carry out capacity building exercises for integrating and monitoring and evaluating gender related issues,
- Collect gender sensitive data based on selected indicators,
- Monitor the progress against targets set for the period under evaluation and feed back results into the system to allow mid-course correction,
- Assess progress and make corrections if needed to obtain gender related outcomes.

Implementation Completion

- Assess impact of gender integration in the overall project context,
- Assess impact of project interventions on men and women
- Derive and share lessons.

As mentioned earlier, we may need to engender the Logframe or the Project Design Summary in order to ensure that gender concerns are built into the project interventions. One of the ways this can be done is by following the model provided by Hambly-Odame (2002):

	Narrative Summary	*Performance Indicators*	*Means of Verification*	*Assumptions*
Goal	Do gender relations influence in any way the goal at the policy level	What measures can verify achievement of the gender sensitive goal	Are data for verifying the goals, objectives, outputs and activities sex-disaggregated and analysed in terms of gender? What gender analysis tools will be appropriate	What important external factors are necessary for sustaining the gender sensitive goal?
Objectives	Does the project have gender responsive objectives?	What measures can verify achievement of the gender responsive objectives?		What important external factors are necessary for sustaining the gender responsive objective?
Outputs	Is the distribution of benefits taking into account gender roles and relations?	What measures can verify that project benefits accrue to women as well as men, and to different groups of women?		What important external factors are necessary for achieving project benefits, especially for women?
Activities	Are gender issues clarified in the implementation of the project	What resources do project beneficiaries contribute to the project? Is the contribution of women as well as men accounted for? Are there external resources that account for women's access and control over resources?		What important external factors are necessary for achieving the activities and especially ensuring continued involvement of men and women in the project?

Outcome Mapping

While most development organizations are under pressure to demonstrate that their programs result in significant and lasting changes in the well-being of large numbers of their intended beneficiaries, such "impacts" are often the product of a confluence of events for which no single agency or group of agencies can realistically claim full credit. A methodology, outcome mapping, has evolved which characterizes and assesses the contributions development programs make to the achievement of outcomes. Outcome mapping can be adapted for use at the project, program, or organizational levels as a monitoring system or it can be used to evaluate on-going or completed activities. It takes a learning-based and use-driven view of evaluation guided by principles of participation and iterative learning, encouraging evaluative thinking throughout the program cycle by all program team members. The focus of outcome mapping is on people and organizations. The originality of the methodology is its shift away from assessing the products of a program (*e.g.*, policy relevance, poverty alleviation, reduced conflict) to focus on changes in behaviours, relationships, actions, and/or activities of the people and organizations with whom a development program works directly.

Elements of Implementation Monitoring	*Elements of Outcome Monitoring*
• Description of the problem or situation before the intervention; • Benchmarks for activities and immediate outputs; • Data collection on inputs, activities and immediate outputs; • Systematic reporting on provision of inputs, etc.; • Directly linked to a discrete intervention (or series of interventions); • Designed to provide information on administrative, implementation and management issues as opposed to broader development effectiveness issues.	• Baseline data to describe the problem or situation before the intervention;• Indicators for outcomes; • Data collection on outputs and how/whether they contribute towards achievement of outcomes; • More focus on perceptions of change among stakeholders and more focus on "soft" assistance; • Systematic reporting with more qualitative and quantitative information on the progress of outcomes; • Done in conjunction with strategic partners; • Captures information on success or failure of strategy.

UNDP Handbook on Monitoring and Evaluation for Results, New York, 2002

This alters the way a program understands its goals and assesses its performance and results. Outcome Mapping establishes a vision of the human, social, and environmental betterment to which the program hopes to contribute and then focuses monitoring and evaluation on factors and actors within its sphere of influence. Development is to be accomplished through changes in the behaviour of people; therefore, this is the central concept of Outcome Mapping. Outcome Mapping focuses on changes in the behaviour of people, groups, and organizations with whom a program works directly. These changes are called "outcomes." Through Outcome Mapping, development programs can claim contributions to the achievement of outcomes rather than claiming the achievement of development impacts. Although these outcomes, in turn, enhance the possibility of development impacts,

	Outcome Monitoring	*Outcome Evaluation*
Objective	To track changes from baseline conditions to desired outcomes.	To validate what results were achieved, and how and why they were or were not achieved
Focus	Focuses on the outputs of projects, programmes, partnerships and soft assistance activities and their contribution to outcomes.	Compares planned with intended outcome achievement. Focuses on how and why outputs and strategies contributed to achievement of outcomes. Focuses on questions of relevance, effectiveness, sustainability and change.
Methodology	Tracks and assesses performance (progress towards outcomes) through analysis and comparison of indicators over time.	Evaluates achievement of outcomes by comparing indicators before and after the intervention. Relies on monitoring data on information from external sources.
Conduct	Continuous and systematic by Programme Managers, Project Managers and key partners.	Time-bound, periodic, in-depth.External evaluators and partners.
Use	Alerts managers to problems in performance, provides options for corrective actions and helps demonstrate accountability.	Provides managers with strategy and policy options, provides basis for learning and demonstrates accountability.

the relationship is not necessarily one of direct cause and effect. Instead of attempting to measure the impact of the program's partners on development, Outcome Mapping concentrates on monitoring and evaluating its results in terms of the influence of the program on the roles these partners play in development.

Outcome Mapping provides a development program with the tools to think holistically and strategically about how it intends to achieve results. The first stage of intentional design helps a program clarify and reach consensus on the changes it would like to support and to plan the strategies. It is only appropriate and useful once a program has chosen its strategic directions and wants, to chart its goals, partners, activities, and progress toward anticipated results. After clarifying the changes the program intends to help bring about, activities are chosen that maximize the likelihood of success. The intentional design stage helps answer four questions: Why? (Vision statement), Who? (Boundary partners), What? (Outcome challenges and progress markers), How? (Mission, strategy maps).

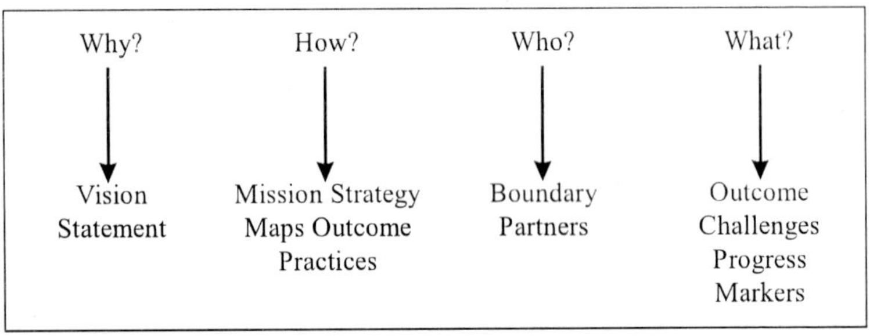

The second stage, outcome and performance monitoring, provides a framework for ongoing monitoring of the program's actions in support of its boundary partners' progress towards the achievement of outcomes. The program uses progress markers, a set of graduated indicators of behavioural change identified in the intentional design stage, to clarify directions with boundary partners and to monitor outcomes (outcome journal). It uses a strategy journal (to monitor strategies and activities) and a performance journal (to monitor organizational practices) to complete a performance-monitoring framework. This framework provides the program the opportunity and tools both to reflect on and improve performance and to collect data on the results of its work with its boundary partners. Whereas with the monitoring framework in Stage 2 the program gathers information that is broad in coverage, a strategic evaluation examines a strategy, issue, or relationship in greater depth. The third stage, evaluation planning, helps the program set evaluation priorities so that it can target evaluation resources and activities where they will be most useful. An evaluation plan outlines the main elements of the evaluations to be conducted.

Empowerment Evaluation: Is one of the latest entrants to the field of evaluation. A wide range of program and policy sectors use empowerment evaluation, including substance abuse prevention, HIV prevention, crime prevention, environmental protection, welfare reform, battered women's shelters, agriculture and rural development, adult probation, adolescent pregnancy prevention, tribal partnership for substance abuse, self-determination and individuals with disabilities, doctoral programs, and educational reform.

Empowerment evaluation is the use of evaluation concepts, techniques, and findings to foster improvement and self-determination. It employs both qualitative and quantitative methodologies. Although it can be applied to individuals, organizations, communities, and societies or cultures, the focus is usually on programs. Empowerment evaluation has an unambiguous value orientation—it is designed to help people help themselves and improve their programs using a form of self-evaluation and reflection. Program participants—including clients—conduct their own evaluations; an outside evaluator often serves as a coach or additional facilitator depending on internal program capabilities.

Empowerment evaluation has three steps. The first step is establishing a mission or vision statement about the program. Some groups do not like the terms mission or vision and instead prefer to focus on results. They state the results they would like to see, based on the outcome of the implemented program—specifying activities required to achieve those processes and outcomes.

The second step, taking stock, involves identifying and prioritizing the most significant program activities. Then program staff members and participants rate how well the program is doing in each of those activities, typically on a 1 (low) to 10 (high) scale, and discuss the ratings. This helps to determine where the program stands, including strengths and weaknesses.

The third step involves charting a course for the future. The group states goals and strategies to achieve their dreams. Goals help program staff members and participants determine where they want to go in the future with an explicit emphasis on program improvement. Strategies help them accomplish program goals. These efforts are monitored using credible documentation. Empowerment evaluators help program staff members and participants identify the type of evidence required to document progress toward their goals. Evaluation becomes a part of the normal planning and management of the program, which is a means of institutionalizing and internalizing evaluation.

Empowerment evaluation is fundamentally a democratic process. The entire group—not a single individual, not the external evaluator or an internal manager—is responsible for conducting the evaluation. The group thus can serve as a check on its own members, moderating the various biases and agendas of individual members. The evaluator is a co-equal in this endeavour, not a superior and not a servant; as a critical friend, the evaluator can question shared biases or "group think".

As is the case in traditional evaluation, everyone is accountable in one fashion or another and thus has an interest or agenda to protect. Empowerment evaluations, like all other evaluations, exist within a context. However, the range of intermediate objectives linking what most people do in their daily routine and macro goals is almost infinite. People often feel empowered and self-determined when they can select intermediate objectives that are linked to larger, global goals. In addition, a self-evaluation is more meaningful when linked to external requirements and demands.

Empowerment evaluation also empowers external evaluators. Specifically, the external evaluator's role and productivity is enhanced by the presence of an empowerment or internal evaluation process. Most evaluators operate significantly below their capacity in an evaluation because the program lacks even rudimentary evaluation mechanisms and processes. The external evaluator routinely devotes time to the development and maintenance of elementary evaluation systems. Programs that already have a basic self-evaluation process in place enable external evaluators to begin operating at a much more sophisticated level.

Universal Declaration of Human Rights—1948

1. When children are born, they are free and each should be treated in the same way. They have reason and conscience and should act towards one another in a friendly manner.
2. Everyone can claim the following rights, despite

   (a) a different sex,
   (b) a different skin colour,
   (c) speaking a different language,
   (d) thinking different things,
   (e) believing in another religion,
   (f) owning more or less,
   (g) being born in another social group,
   (h) coming from another country.

   It also makes no difference whether the country you live in is independent or not.
3. You have the right to live, and to live in freedom and safety.
4. Nobody has the right to treat you as his or her slave and you should not make anyone your slave.
5. Nobody has the right to torture you.
6. You should be legally protected in the same way everywhere, and like everyone else.
7. The law is the same for everyone; it should be applied in the same way to all.
8. You should be able to ask for legal help when the rights your country grants you are not respected. Nobody has the right to put you in prison, to keep you there, or to send you away from your country unjustly, or without a good reason.

9. Nobody has the right to put you in prison, to keep you there, or to send you away from your country unjustly, or without a good reason.
10. If you must go on trial this should be done in public. The people who try you should not let themselves be influenced by others.
11. You should be considered innocent until it can be proved that you are guilty. If you are accused of a crime, you should always have the right to defend yourself. Nobody has the right to condemn you and punish you for something you have not done.
12. You have the right to ask to be protected if someone tries to harm your good name, enter your house, open your letters, or other you or your family without a good reason.
13. You have the right to come and go as you wish within your country. You have the right to leave your country to go to another one; and you should be able to return to your country if you want.
14. If someone hurts you, you have the right to go to another country and ask it to protect you. You lose this right if you have killed someone and if you yourself do not respect what is written here.
15. You have the right to belong to a country and nobody can prevent you, without a good reason, from belonging to another country if you wish.
16. As soon as a person is legally entitled, he or she has the right to marry and have a family. Neither the colour of your skin, nor the country you come from nor should your religion be impediments to doing this. Men and women have the same rights when they are married and also when they are separated. Nobody should force a person to marry. The Government of your country should protect your family and its members.
17. You have the right to own things and nobody has the right to take these from you without a good reason.
18. You have the right to profess your religion freely, to change it, and to practice it either on your own or with other people.

19. You have the right to think what you want, and to say what you like, and nobody should forbid you from doing so. You should be able to share your ideas – also with people from any other country.
20. You have the right to organize peaceful meetings or to take part in meetings in a peaceful way. It is wrong to force someone to belong to a group.
21. You have the right to take part in your country's political affairs either by belonging to the Government yourself of by choosing politicians who have the same ideas as you. Governments should be voted for regularly and voting should be secret. You should get a vote and all votes should be equal. You also have the same right to join the public service as anyone else.
22. The society in which you live should help you to develop and to make the most of all the advantages (culture, work, social welfare) that are offered to you and to all the men and women in your country.
23. You have the right to work, to be free to choose your work, and to get a salary that allows you to live and support your family. If a man and a woman do the same work, they should get the same pay. All people who work have the right to join together to defend their interests.
24. Each work day should not be too long, since everyone has the right to rest and should be able to take regular paid holidays.
25. You have the right to have whatever you need so that you and your family: do not fall ill; do not go hungry; have clothes and a house; and are helped if you are out of work, if you are ill, if you are old, if your wife or husband is dead, or if you do not earn a living for any other reason you cannot help. Both a mother who is going to have a baby and her baby should get special help. All children have the same rights, whether or not the mother is married.
26. You have the right to go to school and everyone should go to school. Primary schooling should be free. You should be able

to learn a profession or continue your studies as far as you wish. At school, you should be able to develop all your talents and you should be taught to get on with others, whatever their race, their religion or the country they come from. Your parents have the right to choose how and what you will be taught at school.

27. You have the right to share in your community's arts and sciences, and in any good they do. Your works as an artist, a writer or a scientist should be protected, and you should be able to benefit from them.
28. To make sure that your rights will be respected, there must be an "order" that can protect them. This "order" should be local and worldwide.
29. You have duties towards the community within which your personality can fully develop. The law should guarantee human rights. It should allow everyone to respect others and to be respected.
30. No society and no human being in any part of the world should act in such a way as to destroy the rights that you have just been reading about.

Declaration on the Right to Development

Adopted by General Assembly Resolution 41/128 of 4 December 1986

The General Assembly,

Bearing in mind the purposes and principles of the Charter of the United Nations relating to the achievement of international co-operation in solving international problems of an economic, social, cultural or humanitarian nature, and in promoting and encouraging respect for human rights and fundamental freedoms for all without distinction as to race, sex, language or religion,

Recognizing that development is a comprehensive economic, social, cultural and political process, which aims at the constant improvement of the well-being of the entire population and of all individuals on the basis of their active, free and meaningful participation in development and in the fair distribution of benefits resulting therefrom,

Considering that under the provisions of the Universal Declaration of Human Rights everyone is entitled to a social and international order in which the rights and freedoms set forth in that Declaration can be fully realized,

Recalling the provisions of the International Covenant on Economic, Social and Cultural Rights and of the International Covenant on Civil and Political Rights,

Recalling further the relevant agreements, conventions, resolutions, recommendations and other instruments of the United Nations and its specialized agencies concerning the integral development of the human being, economic and social progress and development of all peoples, including those instruments concerning decolonization, the prevention of discrimination, respect for and observance of, human rights and fundamental freedoms, the maintenance of international peace and security and the further promotion of friendly relations and co-operation among States in accordance with the Charter,

Recalling the right of peoples to self-determination, by virtue of which they have the right freely to determine their political status and to pursue their economic, social and cultural development,

Recalling also the right of peoples to exercise, subject to the relevant provisions of both International Covenants on Human Rights, full and complete sovereignty over all their natural wealth and resources,

Mindful of the obligation of States under the Charter to promote universal respect for and observance of human rights and fundamental freedoms for all without distinction of any kind such as race, colour, sex, language, religion, political or other opinion, national or social origin, property, birth or other status,

Considering that the elimination of the massive and flagrant violations of the human rights of the peoples and individuals affected by situations such as those resulting from colonialism, neo-colonialism, apartheid, all forms of racism and racial discrimination, foreign domination and occupation, aggression and threats against national sovereignty, national unity and territorial integrity and threats of war would contribute to the establishment of circumstances propitious to the development of a great part of mankind,

Concerned at the existence of serious obstacles to development, as well as to the complete fulfilment of human beings and of peoples, constituted, inter alia, by the denial of civil, political, economic, social and cultural rights, and considering that all human rights and fundamental freedoms are indivisible and interdependent and that, in order to promote development, equal attention and urgent consideration should be given to the implementation, promotion and protection of civil, political, economic, social and cultural rights and that, accordingly, the promotion of, respect for and enjoyment of certain human rights and fundamental freedoms cannot justify the denial of other human rights and fundamental freedoms,

Considering that international peace and security are essential elements for the realization of the right to development,

Reaffirming that there is a close relationship between disarmament and development and that progress in the field of disarmament would considerably promote progress in the field of development and that resources released through disarmament measures should be devoted to the economic and social development and well-being of all peoples and, in particular, those of the developing countries,

Recognizing that the human person is the central subject of the development process and that development policy should therefore make the human being the main participant and beneficiary of development,

Recognizing that the creation of conditions favourable to the development of peoples and individuals is the primary responsibility of their States,

Aware that efforts at the international level to promote and protect human rights should be accompanied by efforts to establish a new international economic order,

Confirming that the right to development is an inalienable human right and that equality of opportunity for development is a prerogative both of nations and of individuals who make up nations,

Proclaims the following Declaration on the Right to Development:

Article 1

1. The right to development is an inalienable human right by virtue of which every human person and all peoples are entitled to participate in, contribute to, and enjoy economic, social, cultural and political development, in which all human rights and fundamental freedoms can be fully realized.
2. The human right to development also implies the full realization of the right of peoples to self-determination, which includes, subject to the relevant provisions of both International Covenants on Human Rights, the exercise of

their inalienable right to full sovereignty over all their natural wealth and resources.

Article 2

1. The human person is the central subject of development and should be the active participant and beneficiary of the right to development.
2. All human beings have a responsibility for development, individually and collectively, taking into account the need for full respect for their human rights and fundamental freedoms as well as their duties to the community, which alone can ensure the free and complete fulfilment of the human being, and they should therefore promote and protect an appropriate political, social and economic order for development.
3. States have the right and the duty to formulate appropriate national development policies that aim at the constant improvement of the well-being of the entire population and of all individuals, on the basis of their active, free and meaningful participation in development and in the fair distribution of the benefits resulting therefrom.

Article 3

1. States have the primary responsibility for the creation of national and international conditions favourable to the realization of the right to development.
2. The realization of the right to development requires full respect for the principles of international law concerning friendly relations and co-operation among States in accordance with the Charter of the United Nations.
3. States have the duty to co-operate with each other in ensuring development and eliminating obstacles to development. States should realize their rights and fulfil their duties in such a manner as to promote a new international economic order based on sovereign equality, interdependence, mutual interest

and co-operation among all States, as well as to encourage the observance and realization of human rights.

Article 4

1. States have the duty to take steps, individually and collectively, to formulate international development policies with a view to facilitating the full realization of the right to development.
2. Sustained action is required to promote more rapid development of developing countries. As a complement to the efforts of developing countries, effective international co-operation is essential in providing these countries with appropriate means and facilities to foster their comprehensive development.

Article 5

States shall take resolute steps to eliminate the massive and flagrant violations of the human rights of peoples and human beings affected by situations such as those resulting from apartheid, all forms of racism and racial discrimination, colonialism, foreign domination and occupation, aggression, foreign interference and threats against national sovereignty, national unity and territorial integrity, threats of war and refusal to recognize the fundamental right of peoples to self-determination.

Article 6

1. All States should co-operate with a view to promoting, encouraging and strengthening universal respect for and observance of all human rights and fundamental freedoms for all without any distinction as to race, sex, language or religion.
2. All human rights and fundamental freedoms are indivisible and interdependent; equal attention and urgent consideration should be given to the implementation, promotion and

protection of civil, political, economic, social and cultural rights.

3. States should take steps to eliminate obstacles to development resulting from failure to observe civil and political rights, as well as economic social and cultural rights.

Article 7

All States should promote the establishment, maintenance and strengthening of international peace and security and, to that end, should do their utmost to achieve general and complete disarmament under effective international control, as well as to ensure that the resources released by effective disarmament measures are used for comprehensive development, in particular that of the developing countries.

Article 8

1. States should undertake, at the national level, all necessary measures for the realization of the right to development and shall ensure, inter alia, equality of opportunity for all in their access to basic resources, education, health services, food, housing, employment and the fair distribution of income. Effective measures should be undertaken to ensure that women have an active role in the development process. Appropriate economic and social reforms should be carried out with a view to eradicating all social injustices.
2. States should encourage popular participation in all spheres as an important factor in development and in the full realization of all human rights.

Article 9

1. All the aspects of the right to development set forth in the present Declaration are indivisible and interdependent and each of them should be considered in the context of the whole.

2. Nothing in the present Declaration shall be construed as being contrary to the purposes and principles of the United Nations, or as implying that any State, group or person has a right to engage in any activity or to perform any act aimed at the violation of the rights set forth in the Universal Declaration of Human Rights and in the International Covenants on Human Rights.

Article 10

Steps should be taken to ensure the full exercise and progressive enhancement of the right to development, including the formulation, adoption and implementation of policy, legislative and other measures at the national and international levels.

Key Questions : Checklist for a Community Profile

Resources

- What are the principle natural resources available to the community?
- Who uses them and how are they used?
- Where are they located?

Livelihoods

- What are the different activities that households in the community use to support their livelihoods?
- Who is involved in those livelihood activities (men/women, young/old, different social and economic groups) and how many people and households depend on them?
- When do those activities take place (time of day/month/seasons) and where?

Community Structure

- How many people and households live in the community?
- What is the gender and age structure of the community?
- What different social, economic, ethnic and cultural groups are there in the community?
- How are those groups defined?
- Where do those different social, economic, ethnic and cultural groups live?

Local Institutions

- What formal organisations and associations are there in the community?

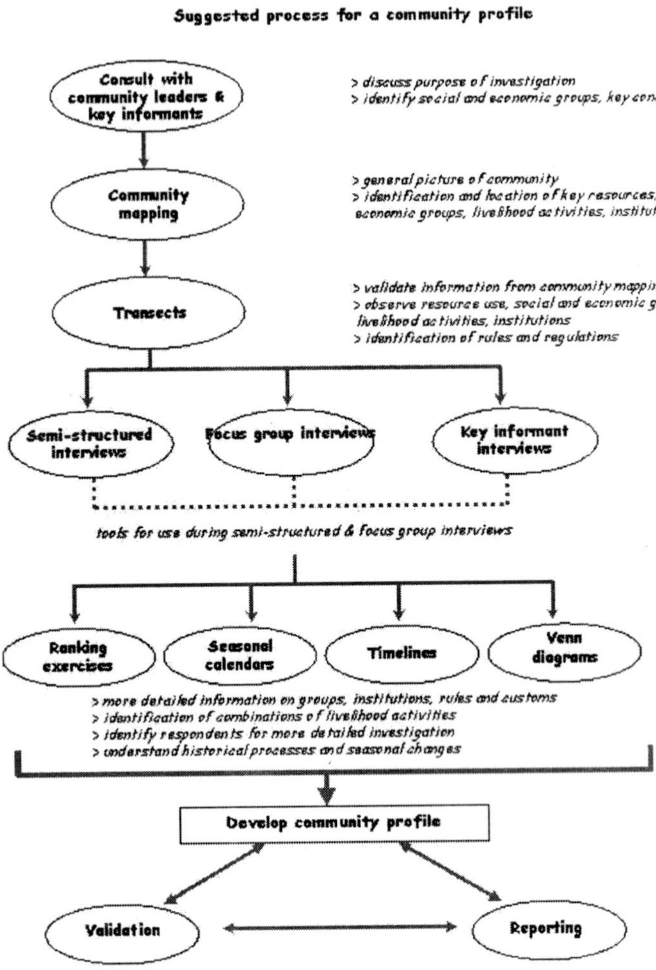

- What rules, regulations and customs are there in place?
- Who is affected by them and how?

Community Infrastructure

- What services are available in the community (transport, power and water supply, markets, agricultural extension, health, education, etc.)?

- Who has access to these services?
- How expensive are the user fees for these services?

Community History

- How long has the community been in existence and how was it founded?
- When did different social, economic, ethnic and cultural groups settle in the community?
- How has the community changed over time and what has caused those changes?

Identifying and Understanding the Poor

Identification of the rural poor has been a contentious as well as challenging issue for development practitioners. Many and varied measurement tools have been developed over a period. The food energy method (FEM) estimates a food energy minimum required to satisfy dietary energy (caloric) requirements and then determines the level of income/consumption at which this is typically met. The cost-of-basic-needs method (CBN) sets the poverty line as the level just sufficient to buy an exogenously set low-cost adequate diet plus other cheap basic requirements. The food-share method (FSM) estimates the minimum cost of a food basket that satisfies the food energy minimum and multiplies this by the share of non-food expenditure in total consumption of a sub-group defined as poor.

It is however important to note that figures arrived at through the above and similar scalar methods mostly reveal only the extent of poverty and not always yield to understanding of the 'poor'. It is interesting also that some of the poor are not poor all the time. The transient poor are therefore to be treated differently from the chronic poor. Poverty varies in time in other ways. (a) Depth of chronic poverty varies over time. (b) Absolute poverty may be more likely to be transient than relative poverty, *i.e.* being poorest may be more persistent than being absolutely poor. (c) Some who make the transition out of poverty fall back: how much transient poverty reflects people who repeatedly move above and below the poverty line; how much of poverty is just a one-off incident; or do the same unfortunate people suffer may incidents? (IFAD 2001)

Answers to the above questions have a bearing, as they would ultimately determine the nature and quality of interventions. The following table illustrates the differences in the condition of the poor and the absolutely poor, very appropriately. The nature and quality of interventions for the two groups would be dependent on our understanding of their objective reality.

Characteristics of the Poor and Very Poor: an Indonesian Example

Indicator	*Absolutely poor*	*Poor*
Food Sufficiency & Purchase	Food insufficient More than 70% income spent on food Needs to borrow for food-purchase	Food slightly insufficient About 50% income spent on food Occasional borrowing for food purchase
Land Holdings	No land or shareholder High rent paid on shareholding	Small owner cum shareholder
Agricultural input use occasionally	No purchased inputs used except that received via aid	Fertiliser and pesticides used
Labour utilization and employment	Only family labour used Seasonal employment	Occasional use of hired labour More regular employment
Use of utilities	Not available Use non-mechanised source of drinking water	Few utilities available Availability of mechanised source of drinking water
House and Ownership	Simple house with earthen floor and thatched roof	Simple house of wood and thatch with earthen floor
Children's Education	Never attend school or never graduate from primary	Primary schooling
Literacy of parents	Both illiterate	One parent able to read and write
Vehicle/Transport	None or one bicycle Occasionally able to afford public transport	One or more bicycle Able to afford public transport most of the time
Livestock (less poultry)	None	Only small ruminants
Valued goods	Maximum two-bad radio No jewellery or gold	Two or four band radio Few pieces of jewellery or gold
Cooking material	Firewood and very rarely kerosene	Firewood and kerosene
Health access	Only traditional healer during emergencies	Traditional healer and formal health service for serious illness
Income source	Exclusively from agricultural activities	About 10-25% income supplemented from non-farm activities
Distance from house to market	More than 10 Km with difficult access	Within 10 Km and relatively easily accessed
Family size	More than 6	Less than 6.

The moot question then is how we, as practitioners, identify the real poor. As mentioned earlier, the Govt. of India follows a poverty—line whereby, the poor are defined as those earning less than a per capita monthly expenditure of Rs.49 for rural areas and Rs.57 in urban areas at 1973-74 all India prices. This poverty line corresponds to a total household per capita expenditure sufficient to provide, in addition to basic non-food items-clothing, transport—a daily intake of 2400 calories per person in rural areas and 2100 in urban areas. The income/consumption method, defines well-being in terms of basic needs-satisfaction, proxied by income or consumption expenditure levels obtained from household survey data. This approach relies on naturalistic epistemological and ethical underpinnings, *i.e.* the application of methods of enquiry used in the natural science to the social sciences. On the other hand, the participatory approach has close epistemological and ethical affinities with critical hermeneutics, *i.e.* the study of social meaning with a view to expose delusion and empower. It is critical to understand that different conceptual frameworks to poverty yield different results. Divergent results were obtained from studies based on income consumption and participatory approaches; the principal area of divergence being gender and poverty. The participatory study concluded that women constitute the most disadvantaged segment of Guinean society. The income/consumption study did not. (See also, Paul Shaffer 1995).

Most practitioners are committed to serve and work with the poorest-of-the-poor. However, with all their intentions and efforts to do so, they often come to the realization at the end of the project, that they have left out the real poor.

Participatory Poverty Assessment (PPA): has been defined as an iterative, participatory research process that seeks to understand poverty from the perspective of a range of stakeholders, especially the poor (Narayan, 2001). PPA seeks to understand poverty in its social, institutional, and political context. It recognizes that other aspects of deprivation and well-being, such as dignity, respect within the community, love and religion may be equally, if not more, important for the poor in determining their livelihood strategies.

The basic principles of PPA underpin the approach.

1. Poverty must be analysed and understood in a holistic fashion;
2. The perceptions of the poor, themselves, must be incorporated in poverty assessments;
3. The role of the poor as researchers and planners must be recognized and they must be actively engaged in identifying the causal factors of poverty and in planning poverty alleviation strategies; Other stakeholders must also be involved in the process if lasting solutions are to be found; and
4. PPA's can contain hard data too.

PPA helps us to understand poverty in its various dimensions, viz:

(a) The views of the poor, their different priorities and choices.
(b) Gender differences in social norms, violence, and empowerment; as well as in employment, status, politics, and entitlements.
(c) Complexity of poverty, *i.e.* its variability over time, season; role of financial, natural, physical, political, social, and human assets & role of institutions and laws.
(d) Subjective views of poverty: insecurity, isolation, powerlessness, lack of respect, and lack of freedom.
(e) How the poor cope with poor basic infrastructure, corrupt officials and stock & contingencies.

In order to understand poverty holistically, we need information on many immeasurable aspects like access to resources & services, the role of institutions and social networks in people's lives and seasonal fluctuations in vulnerability. A range of participatory and open-ended methods is used to gain understanding of such and other related factors. PPA is not necessarily qualitative; it uses and complements quantitative methods. Some of the methods used in the PPA area the traditional Participatory Rural Appraisal (PRA); Rapid Rural Appraisal (RRA); Self-esteem, associative strength, resourcefulness, action planning and responsibility (SARAR); semi-structured interviews; and focused group discussions etc. Some of the issues that have emerged through PPA's an how their coverage differs from conventional methods are given below (IFAD, 2001)

Issues	*Aspects addressed through PPA*	*Aspects addressed by conventional methods*
Sanitation	Lack of access to clean water and toilets	Presence or absence of hand pump or water point with very little information about the working condition
Corruption	How corrupt officials can prevent poor people from obtaining facilities that they are entitled to	Not usually addressed by poverty surveys
Definitions of Poverty	How the poor understand, define, interpret poverty, its causes and effects	Poverty defined in terms of nutritional intake or income/ expenditure
Risk and Vulnerability	What kind of events could pose a threat to livelihood patterns and what coping mechanisms the poor employ	Not covered in depth by poverty surveys
Access	Access to services, institutions infrastructure, common property resources	Yields or physical structures are taken as proxy for access and availability

Illustrative Techniques

Participatory Wealth Ranking (PWR): PWR is a modification of the PRA technique. It is a subjective and local ranking of wealth used by members of a community in order to establish which members within the community are more destitute. Community members generate their own criteria with which to rank poverty or wealth; this often includes factors that are not visible or easily identified by an outsider. By engaging the community members throughout the process, people are empowered to analyse their own situations, often giving them greater ownership in the programmes that are established to help the poorest in the communities.

Indicative Wealth Ranking Reference Sheet

Indicators	*Community Ranking*					
	Surplus	*Self Sufficient*	*Moderately Poor*	*Subsistence*	*Very Poor*	*Destitute*
Housing	Pucca-owned	Pucca or mixed-owned	Mixed or Kutcha-owned	Kutcha-own or rented or other arrangement	Very poor quality Kutcha-owned or rented or other arrangement	Shelter in others house, no owned place
Rooms	Adequate	Small but manageable	Manageable	Inadequate-crowding	Inadequate-crowding	Inadequate-crowding
General Condition	Good	Manageable, may need little repairs	Needs repairs, annually	Needs repair or improvement to make it worth living	Needs repair-unconducive	Needs repair-unconducive
Income	Ensured source	Ensured source	Less income than requirement, no ensured source	No ensured source	No ensured source, mostly wage earning, temporary, seasonal	Wage, bonded labour, begging, may be physically handicapped
	More than 1 source	At least 1 ensured source	Wage labour, temporary work, small petty business	Temporary work, wage labour, small petty business	Earning not sufficient to meet daily household requirements	
	Often surplus gene-	Earning enough to	Takes loan at the time	Struggle to manage,	Struggle hard to	Cannot arrange

(contd.)

(contd.)

Indicators	*Community Ranking*					
	Surplus	*Self Sufficient*	*Moderately Poor*	*Subsistence*	*Very Poor*	*Destitute*
	related	manage the family, may not be generating surplus	of requirement	takes loan quite often from different sources	maintain the family, usually takes loans to manage the family, seasonal migration	food on daily basis depends on others for food
Food habits	Getting quality food	Getting good food	Manage to arrange a square meal a day, not qualitative food	Manage to arrange a square meal a day, but very often face a problem	Difficult to arrange a square meal a day	
	No problem in arranging food	No problem in arranging food	Sometime face problem in arranging food	High consumption requirement	High consumption requirement	
Status in the Community	Respectable before others in the community	Respectable before others in the community	Not much respect, a general villager	A common villager	A common villager, may be looked at with pity	
	Take part in community decision making	Take part in community decision making	Not recognized as an important member of the community			
Dependents	Less dependents	Less dependents	More dependents	More number of dependents in the family	More number of dependents in the family	

(contd.)

(contd.)

Indicators	*Community Ranking*					
	Surplus	*Self Sufficient*	*Moderately Poor*	*Subsistence*	*Very Poor*	*Destitute*
	More income than dependents	More income than dependents	Less income to feed more dependents, Less earning members in the family	Less income to feed more dependents, Less earning members in the family	income to feed more dependents, Less earning members in the family	
Assets	Television, Almirah, Bicycle or other high cost assets	Television, Almirah, Bicycle or other high cost assets	Only bicycle, radio, watch etc.	No assets except basic household utensils	No assets except basic household utensils	No household assets

CASHPOR House Index (CHI): is an external, observational methodology, which provides a cost-effective way to identify very poor people. The CHI entails looking at seven main features of a house, including size, number of stories, structural condition, building materials used for walls and roofing, utility supply, and ownership of vehicles. These criteria are adapted as necessary to suit local situations. Each component is allocated points. A cut-off score is set so that families whose houses score above a certain number of points are not eligible for participation in the credit programme, while households that score below the certain number of points become eligible for further consideration. An appeals process if established for families who claim to be very poor but whose houses score too high to be considered for the programme.

The Housing Index uses the structure of the house and sometimes the compound to differentiate between economic levels of households and identify those who are poor. Since housing is generally the most important asset of households and since people generally invest a great deal in their houses, the building itself represents an extremely visible reflection of household wealth.

The size of the house and compound, the material used for building the house, the number of rooms, the presence of running water and bathroom facilities, all taken together provide very strong impressionistic evidence of household economic levels. The housing index, variations of which are used by several MFIs, but which has been standardized best by CASHPOR, uses these features to determine who is poor and who is better off.

Field staff walks systematically through villages or sections of villages. They look at each house, eliminating those that are obviously expensive and well built. The others are scored according to size, construction materials for walls, floor and roof, and sometimes other variables such as water supply, toilets, and access to electricity, etc. Scores for each indicator are then added to create a composite score. Cutoff scores are established to include households considered poor and exclude those that are well off.

CASHPOR has been a pioneer in developing the Housing Index (www.cashpor.com). It created a composite index known as the CASHPOR House Index using the size of the house, its structural condition, the quality of walls, and the quality of the roof. It scores houses based on:

1. Size
   Small: 0, Medium: 2, Big: 6,
2. Structural condition
   Dilapidated: 0, Average: 2, Good 6,
3. Quality of walls
   Poor: 0, Average: 2, Good: 6,
4. Quality of roof
   Thatch/Leaves: 0, Tin/Iron sheets: 2, Permanent roof: 6.

A cut-off score of total points is established to separate the houses of the poor from those of the non-poor. The index is context specific and CASHPOR has refined its index for adaptation to different regions.

The characteristics MFIs consider to create their housing indices can be quite minimum to being relatively extensive. TSPI in Philippines has a fairly simple housing index. It scores houses based on:

(1) Size (Big: 4, Medium: 2, Small: 0)
(2) Structure (Firm: 4, Moderate: 2, Bad: 0), and
(3) Roof (Tiles: 2, New: 1, Old: 0.5 and Nipa: 0).

SHARE in India, on the other hand, brings into account quite extensive housing characteristics in computing the housing index. It scores houses based on:

(1) Size (Big: 4, Medium: 2, Small 0)
(2) Structure (Firm: 4, Medium: 2, Bad: 0)
(3) Roof material (RCC: 4, Tiles: 3, Asbestos: 2, Zinc:1, Bamboo: 0, Thatched: 0, Wood+ Stone + Mud: 1)
(4) Wall material (Brick: 4, Stone: 1, Zinc: 1, Mud: 0.5, Bamboo: 0)
(5) Electric supply (Yes: 2, Shared: 1, No: 0)
(6) Water supply (Own well: 1, Community well: 0)
(7) House Ownership: (Own: 3, Inherited: 2, Rented: 1, Shared: 0)
(8) Toilet (Pit: 2, Flush: 1, Open area: 0)
(9) Cooking (Gas: 3, Oil: 2, Charcoal: 1, Wood: 0, Smokeless Chulhas: 0)
(10) Radio/Tape Recorder (New: 2, Old: 1, None: 0)
(11) Vehicle (New moped: 4, Old Moped: 2, New bicycle: 1, Old bicycle: 0.5, None: 0)
(11) Government Ration Card (Yes: 3, Yellow: 2, White: 1, No: 0)
(13) Fan (Yes: 1, No: 0).

A cut-off score of total points is established to separate the houses of the poor from those of the non-poor. In the case of TSPI an individual with a score below 4.5 is eligible for a loan (although adjustments to that cutoff point are made based on the locality). Individuals with scores of more than 20 are considered ineligible for SHARE loans; while those with scores below 20 are interviewed further to assess their eligibility.

Each eligible household, based on results of the CHI, is subjected to a Networth test. Networth (wealth) is calculated by subtracting the value of the household's debts from the value of the household's major assets. The networth test provides an additional quality check on the results of the CHI and assists in provides the ability to distinguish between poor households and very poor households, with low cost. As local staff has to be involved, the criterion etc. can be locally adapted to maintain objectivity. However, when the CHI is applied to areas where the government has provided the housing or the housing is uniform, it loses some of its ability. Therefore it is important to monitor procedures so as to find any weak implementation or less committed staff who may allow the non-poor to become eligible.obtaining baseline information on potential clients.

Indicative Community Baseline Indicators

I. Household Composition

Size of household	Sex Ratio
Position of respondents	Percentage of dependent members/ earning members
Caste-wise distribution of households	Percentage of children involved in household work and its ratio for male: female children
Percentage of child labour	Poverty Category: Percentage of landless, marginal farmers, small farmers and others
Percentage of infirm or disabled children	Percentage of women engaged only in household work
Activity status of sample households	Ratio of married: unmarried women respondents
Relation between religion and size of households	Percentage of households not having any dependent members
Percentage of divorcee, separated, abandoned among the married respondents	

II. Literacy

Percentage of school going children and its ratio for both boys and girls	Percentage of children enrolled and dropped-out and its ratio for both boys and girls
Literacy level	Percentage of girls who were married before the age of 12 yrs/18 yrs
Most common reasons for children dropping-out of school	Percentage of villages where schools were not existing
Drop-outs among boys and girls	Percentage of females who are illiterate in the age group of 5-20, 20-45 yrs and 45 yrs
Relation between religion and literacy level	Relation between religion and girls education
Relation between marital status and illiteracy	Percentage of illiterate members (male + female)

II. Literacy (contd.)	
Percentage of literate members (male + female) Ratio of literate members: male: female	Ratio of illiteracy – male: female
III. Employment	
Percentage of respondents involved in main occupation to subsidiary occupation	Block specific main and subsidiary occupation among the sample households
Average person days employment available to respondents who are engaged in both main and subsidiary occupation	Average person days employment available to respondents under main occupation
Average person days employment available to respondents under subsidiary occupation	Percentage of respondents involved in main occupation
Percentage of respondents involved only in main or subsidiary occupation.	Percentage of respondents involved in both main & subsidiary occupation
Percentage of respondents employed only 3 months in a year	Percentage of respondents employed only for 3-6 months in a year
Percentage of respondents employed only for 6-9 months in a year	Percentage of respondents employed for more than 9 months in a year
Co-relation between average days employment and poverty category	Co-relation between average days employment and poverty category
Relation between size of households and poverty category	Relation between marital status and employment
Percentage of women below the age of 20 years, who are wage earners	Percentage of women above 45 yrs who are wage earners
Most prevalent occupation among the sample households	Percentage of sample members depending on agriculture (cultivation)
Percentage of sample members who were agri labourers and wage labourers	Percentage depending upon animal husbandry, bee-keeping & sericulture
Percentage involved in handloom and handicrafts, rural artisan	Percentage involved in mineral/metal based and chemical based industries
Percentage involved in forest based industries and collection of MFP	Percentage involved in shop/trading/ wending and transport
Percentage involved in service	
IV. Health Status	
First – three most serious illnesses among males and females	Most prevalent diseases among male adults, female adults, male child and female child

IV. Health Status (contd.)

Percentage of households having no ailment for males and females	Percentage of households having maximum 3 ailments for males and females
Most common mode of treatment followed for minor ailments in case of male children, female children, male adult and female adult	Most common mode of treatment followed for major ailments in case of male children, female children, male adult and female adults
Percentage of households that had infant mortality (male & female)	Percentage of households which had maternal mortality
Percentage of women who availed of anti-tetanus during pregnancy	Percentage of women who did not take anti-tetanus during pregnancy
Percentage of women who did not avail of anti-tetanus due to ignorance, did not believe in taking anti-tetanus, economic factor, facility not available and others	Percentage of households reporting death due to accident (male and female) during last one year.
Percentage of people who committed suicide (male and female)	Percentage of people who died due to fire accident (male and female)
	Percentage of people who died due to other reasons (male and female)

V. Access to Minimum Needs

Percentage of respondents who have to walk long distances to fetch water	Percentage of respondents who have to walk long distances to graze animals
Percentage of respondents who do not have a fair shop in the village	Percentage of respondents who do not send their children to school
Percentage of respondents who do not have all weather roads	The most common drudgery faced by women (in percentage)
Percentage of households which had toilet facilities	Percentage of households having multiple sources of drinking water
Percentage of households who used toilet facilities	Percentage of households having pong/tank, river/spring/lake as source of drinking water
Percentage of households having only one source of drinking water	Percentage of households having access of drinking water in basti
Percentage of households having handpump, tubewell, dugwell	Percentage of households having access to drinking water within 1 km
Percentage of households having access to drinking water in their premises	Percentage of households having access to drinking water more than 2 kms away
Percentage of households having access to drinking water in the outskirts of the village	Percentage of households who used coal, gas, kerosene and bio-gas

V. Access to Minimum Needs (contd.)	
Percentage of households having access to drinking water within 1-2 kms	Percentage of households using one type of fuel alone
Most commonly used fuel by the sample households (in percentage)	Percentage of households using more than one type of fuel
VI. Food Security & Nutrition Status	
Consumption pattern among the adults in the sample households	Consumption pattern among the children in sample households
Extent of food scarcity	Month of food scarcity
Attempt made resorted to, during food scarcity	Frequency of hunger
The most affected category of HH members during shortage of food	Distribution pattern of sample households by their frequency of use of packaged food items
Percentage of respondents not using any package food	Percentage of respondents who used only one item
Percentage of respondents who used two items	Percentage of respondents who used only one item
Percentage of respondents who used more than three items	Distribution of the respondents versus male working members in the sample households by time use
VII. Gender Focused Issues	
Percentage of respondents who come to groom's place before the age of 18	Percentage of respondents who were of the opinion that girls should be married below 15 yrs
Percentage of respondents who were aware of the legal age of marriage of boys and girls	Percentage of respondents who were of the opinion that girls should be married above 18 yrs
Percentage of respondents who were not able to state correct marriageable age for boys and girls	Percentage of respondents who were of the opinion that girls should be married between 16-18 yrs
Percentage of respondents who believed that girls should be educated only: Upto Primary Upto Middle Upto Higher Secondary & above Who do not know	Percentage of respondents who were able to decide on their own, regarding casting their vote
Percentage of respondents who stated that girls have equal right in parents property	Percentage of respondents who did not vote
Extent of mobility among the respondents within and outside the village	Prevalence of different grass-root level institutions in project villages

VII. Gender Focused Issues (contd.)	
Percentage of respondents who were influenced by outsiders regarding voting	Percentage of respondents who leave their children with siblings at home while away at work
Extent of participation of respondents in various social and political institutions	Distribution of respondents by their level of awareness about different social issues
Percentage of respondents who leave their children with elders at home while away at work	Extent of awareness of respondents about different social issues
Percentage of respondents who leave their children with neighbours at home while away at work	Awareness of women regarding their rights
VIII. Access & Control Profile	
Assets in a household on which the respondent has got ownership, access only, control only, ownership + access + control, ownership + access, ownership + control	Only access and control of assets by respondents (in %)
Access and control of assets by respondents + spouse (in %)	Access and control of assets by all family members (in %)
Access and control of assets by outsiders (in %)	
IX. Women's Say in Decision Making	
Purchase or sale of fixed assets	Purchase or sale of moveable assets
sending children to school	Periodic vaccination to children
X. Relationship with Natal Family	
percentage of respondents who do not have the right to visit their parental home whenever they desire	Percentage of respondents who have never visited their parental home
percentage of respondents who frequently visit their parental home (*i.e.* thrice and more than three times)	Three most important occasions when the respondent makes a visit to her native home town (in %)
Care takers of the household during the respondents absence (in %)	Maximum and the minimum duration by which the respondent can keep herself away from the household (in no. of days)
XI. Community Action	
Common injustice faced by women	

XII. Awareness and Benefit availed under Development Programme	
Percentage of respondents who were aware of 1 or more programme Percentage of respondents who have received assistance in the form of Training;	Percentage of respondents who have received benefits Tool Kit; Loan Asset; Subsidy; Revolving Fund etc.
XIII. Skill Base	
Per cent possessing traditional skills Per cent of respondents who found the training in IGA useful for income generation	Per cent who were able to generate income from these skill Per cent of respondents who had obtained training in any skill development for IGA
XIV. Household Expenditure	
Item-wise % to overall monthly expenditure of the household	
XV. Source-wise Annual Income	
Average annual income from various sources Respondents share of income to total household income	Per cent share of income from various sources of the total income Respondents control over income
XVI. Savings Pattern	
Per cent of respondents who are saving Per cent of different types of savings done by the respondents Per cent of household where the done encourages savings habits of his wife	Per cent of respondents who save > 50, 50-100, <100 per month respectively Per cent of household where the husband was aware of the wife's saving habit
XVII. Borrowing Pattern	
Per cent of respondents who had borrowed money Frequency of borrowing (in %) The most prevalent interest rate Per cent levied upon loans availed	Per cent of respondents who had borrowed money just 12 months before Percentage of household having outstanding debt to be re-paid
XVIII. Migration	
Per cent of household members who are migrating	Purpose of migration

XVIII. Migration (contd.)	
Effect of migration on the household	Per cent of people who were able to save from their earnings through migration
Percent of respondents who said that migration : Helped them in purchasing a house Helped them in purchase of land Improved their quality of life Have led to better education of children Others	Per cent of respondents who said that migration have negative effects like : Parents felt neglected Work load on females increased Children's education affected Others

XIX. Time Use Profile
Time spent by the women members for income generating activities, other household activities and childcare as compared to the male members.

A Conceptual Framework for Gender Analysis and Planning

A. The Harvard Analytical Framework: The Harvard Analytical Framework is also called the Gender Roles Framework or Gender Analysis Framework. Developed by the Harvard Institute for International development in collaboration with the WID office of USAID, and based on the WID efficiency approach, it is one of the earliest gender analysis and planning frameworks.

Aims of the Harvard Framework

- To demonstrate that there is an economic rationale for investing in women as well as men.
- To assist planners design more efficient projects and improve overall productivity.
- To emphasise the importance of better information as the basis for meeting the efficiency/equity goal.
- To map the work of men and women in the community and highlight the key differences.

Features

The Harvard framework is originally outlined in Overholt, Anderson, Cloud and Austin, *Gender Roles in Development Projects: A Case Book*, 1984, Kumarian Press: Connecticut.

The framework consists of a matrix for collecting data at the micro (community and household) level. It has four interrelated components:

- the activity profile, which answers the question, "who does what?", including gender, age, time spent and location of the activity.

- the access and control profile, which identifies the resources used to carry out the work identified in the activity profile, and access to and control over their use, by gender.
- the analysis of influencing factors, which charts factors that influence gender differences in the above two profiles.
- the project cycle analysis, which examines a project or intervention in light of gender-disaggregated information.

The framework also contains a series of checklists consisting of key questions to ask at each stage of the project cycle: identification, design, implementation, and evaluation.

CHECKLIST 1: Women's dimension in project identification

Assessing Women's Needs

1. What needs and opportunities exist for increasing women's productivity and/or production?

    - What needs and opportunities exist for increasing women's access to and control of resources?
    - What needs and opportunities exist for increasing women's access to and control of benefits?
    - How do these needs and opportunities relate to the country's other general and sectoral development needs and opportunities?
    - Have women been directly consulted in identifying such needs and opportunities?

Defining General Project Objectives

1. Are project objectives explicitly related to women's needs?

    - Do these objectives adequately reflect women's needs?
    - Have women participated in setting those objectives?
    - Have their been any earlier efforts?
    - How has the present proposal built on earlier activity?

Identifying Possible Negative Effects

1. Might the project reduce women's access to or control of resources and benefits?

   - Might it adversely affect women's situation in some other way?
   - What will be the effects on women in the short and longer term?

CHECKLIST 2: Women's dimension in project design

Project Impact on Women's Activities

1. Which of these activities (Production, reproduction and maintenance, socio-political) does the project affect?

   - Is the planned component consistent with the current gender denomination for the activity?
   - If it is planned to change the women's performance of that activity, *i.e.,* locus of activity, remunerative mode, technology, mode of activity is this feasible, and what positive or negative effects would there be on women?
   - If it does not change, is this a missed opportunity for women's roles in the development process?
   - How can the project design be adjusted to increase the above-mentioned positive effects, and reduce or eliminate the negative ones?

Project Impact on Women's Access and Control

1. How will each of the project components affect women's access to and control of the resources and benefits engaged in and stemming from the production of goods and services?

   - How will each of the project components affect women's access to and control of the resources and benefits engaged in and stemming from the reproduction and maintenance of the human resources?

- How will each of the project components affect women's access to and control of the resources and benefits engaged in and stemming from the socio-political functions?
- What forces have been set into motion to induce further exploration of constraints and possible improvements?
- How can the project design be adjusted to increase women's access to and control of resources and benefits?

CHECKLIST 3: Women's dimension in project implementation

Personnel

1. Are project personnel aware of and sympathetic to women's needs?

    - Are women used to deliver the goods and services to women beneficiaries?
    - Do personnel have the necessary skills to provide any special inputs required by women?
    - What training techniques will be used to develop delivery systems?
    - Are there appropriate opportunities for women to participate in project management positions?

Organisational Structures

1. Does the organisational form enhance women's access to resources?

    - Does the organisation have adequate power to obtain resources needed by women from other organisations?
    - Does the organisation have the institutional capability to support and protect women during the change process?

Operations and Logistics

1. Are the organisation's delivery channels accessible to women in terms of personnel, location and timing?

    - Do control procedures exist to ensure dependable delivery of the goods and services?
    - Are there mechanisms to ensure that the project resources or benefits are not usurped by males?

Finances

1. Do funding mechanisms exist to ensure programme continuity?

    - Are funding levels adequate for proposed tasks?
    - Is preferential access to resources by males avoided?
    - Is it possible to race funds for women from allocation to delivery with a fair deal of accuracy?

Flexibility

1. Does the project have a management information system which will allow it to detect the effects of the operation on women?

    - Does the organisation have enough flexibility to adapt its structures and operations to meet the changing or new-found situations of women?

CHECKLIST 4: Women's dimension in project evaluation

Data Requirements

1. Does the project's monitoring and evaluation system explicitly measure the project's effects on women?

- Does it also collect data to update the Activity Analysis and the Women's Access and Control Analysis?
- Are women involved in designing the data requirements?

Data Collection and Analysis

1. Are the data collected with sufficient frequency so that necessary project adjustments could be made during the project?

    - Are the data fed back to project personnel and beneficiaries in an understandable form and on a timely basis to allow project adjustments?
    - Are women involved in the collection and interpretation of data?
    - Are data analysed so as to provide guidance to the design of other projects?
    - Are key areas of WID research identified?

[Checklists adapted from Overholt, Anderson, Cloud and Austin, *Gender Roles in Development Projects*, Kumarian Press, Connecticut, 1985.]

Uses of the Framework

- Best suited for project planning, rather than programme or policy planning.
- As a gender-neutral entry point when raising gender issues with constituents resistant to considering gender relations and power dynamics.
- For baseline data collection.
- In conjunction with Moser's framework, to draw in the idea of strategic gender needs.

Strengths of the Harvard Framework

- It is practical and hands-on.

- Once the data have been collected, it gives a clear picture of who does what, when and with what resources. It makes women's role and work visible.
- It distinguishes between access to and control over resources.
- It can be easily adapted to a variety of settings and situations.
- It is relatively non-threatening, because it relies on "facts" only.

Potential limitations

- Based on WID (efficiency) rationale, which aims at increasing project/programme efficiency. It does not delineate power relations or decision-making processes. Therefore, the framework offers little guidance on how to change existing gender inequalities. It tends to result in gender-neutral or gender-specific interventions, rather than those that can transform existing gender relations.
- Tends to oversimplify, based on a somewhat superficial, tick-the-boxes approach to data collection, ignoring complexities in the community; may result in lost opportunities for change.
- Is basically a top-down planning tool, excluding women's and men's own analysis of their situation.
- Ignores other underlying inequalities, such as class, race and ethnicity, encouraging an erroneous view of men and women as homogeneous categories.
- Emphasises separation of activities and resources based on sex or age, ignoring connections and co-operative relations across these categories. This can result in projects that may misbehave or cannot tackle women's strategic gender needs.
- The profiles yield a somewhat static view of the community, without reference to changes over time in gender relations.

[Adapted from *Training Workshop for Trainers in Women, Gender and Development, June 9-21, 1996*, Programme Handbook, Royal Tropical Institute, The Netherlands.]

B. Moser's Gender Planning Framework

One of the most popularly used frameworks is that developed by Caroline Moser. It is based on her concepts of gender roles and gender needs, and policy approaches to gender and development planning. Other sections in this module discuss the concepts of gender roles and gender needs, and contain exercises which clarify an understanding of these concepts.

Moser categorises the main policy approaches to women and development as follows:

Policy approaches to low-income Third World women have shifted over the past decade, mirroring shifts in macro-economic development policies. Five different policy approaches can be identified, each categorised in terms of the roles of women on which it focuses and the practical and strategic needs it meets.

- *Welfare*: Earliest approach, 1950-70. Its purpose is to bring women into development as better mothers. Women are seen as passive beneficiaries of development. It recognises the reproductive role of women and seeks to meet PGNs in that role through top-down handouts of food aid, measures against malnutrition and family planning. It is non-challenging and, therefore, still widely popular.
- *Equity*: The original WID approach, used in the 1976-85 UN Women's Decade. Its purpose is to gain equity for women, who are seen as active participants in development. It recognises the triple role and seeks to meet SGNs through direct state intervention giving political and economic autonomy, and reducing inequality with men. It challenges women's subordinate position. It is criticised as Western feminism, is considered threatening, and is unpopular with governments.
- *Anti-poverty*: The second WID approach, a toned-down version of equity, adopted from the 1970s onwards. Its purpose is

to ensure that poor women increase their productivity. Women's poverty is seen as a problem of underdevelopment, not of subordination. It recognises the productive role of women, and seeks to meet the PGN to earn an income, particularly in small-scale income-generating projects. It is most popular with NGOs.

- *Efficiency*: The third, and now predominant, WID approach, adopted particularly since the 1980s debt crisis. Its purpose is to ensure that development is more efficient and effective through women's economic contribution, with participation often equated with equity. It seeks to meet PGNs while relying on all three roles and an elastic concept of women's time. Women are seen entirely in terms of their capacity to compensate for declining social services by extending their working day, very popular approach.
- *Empowerment*: The most recent approach, articulated by Third World women. Its purpose is to empower women through greater self-reliance. Women's subordination is experienced not only because of male oppression but also because of colonial and neo-colonial oppression. It recognises the triple role, and seeks to meet SGNs indirectly through bottom-up mobilisation of PGNs. It is potentially challenging, although its avoidance of Western feminism makes it unpopular except with Third World women's NGOs.

Uses of the Framework

- For planning at all levels from policies to projects.
- In conjunction with Harvard framework.

Strengths of Moser's Framework

- Moves beyond technical elements of planning, recognising its political elements and assuming conflict of interests in the planning process. Recognises the transformative potential of gender planning.
- Conceptualises planning as aiming to challenge unequal gender relations and support women's empowerment.

- Makes all work visible and valuable to planners, through the concept of triple roles.
- Distinguishes between types of gender needs: those that relate to women's daily lives but maintain existing gender relations (practical gender needs), and those potentially transform existing gender subordination (strategic gender needs).
- Categorises policy approaches.

Potential limitations

- The idea of gender roles obscures the notion of gender relationships and can give the false impression of natural order and equality.
- The framework does not mention other forms of inequality, such as class, race or ethnicity.
- The framework is static and does not examine change over time as a variable.
- The policy approaches should not be seen as mutually exclusive; they may often overlap each other in practice.

[Adapted from *Training Workshop for Trainers in Women, Gender and Development, June 9-21, 1996*, Programme Handbook, Royal Tropical Institute, The Netherlands.]

C. Women's Empowerment Framework

This framework was developed by Sara Hlupekile, a gender expert from Lusaka, Zambia.

Aims of the Framework

- To achieve women's empowerment by enabling women to achieve equal control over the factors of production and participate equally in the development process.

Features

Longwe argues that poverty arises not from lack of productivity but from oppression and exploitation. She conceptualises five progressive levels of equality, arranged in hierarchical order, with each higher level denoting a higher level of empowerment. These are the basis to assess the extent of women's empowerment in any area of social or economic life. The levels of equality are:

Control	Using the participation of women in the decision-making process to achieve balance of control between men and women over the factors of production, without one in a position of dominance.
Participation	Pertains to women's equal participation in the decision-making process, policy-making, planning and administration. In development projects, it includes involvement in needs assessment, project design, implementation and evaluation.
Conscientisation	Pertains to an understanding of the difference between sex roles and gender roles and the belief that gender relations and the gender division of labour should be fair and agreeable to both sides, and not based on the domination of one over the other.
Access	Pertains to women's access to factors of production? land, labour, credit, training, marketing facilities, and all publicly available services and benefits? on an equal basis with men. Equality of access is obtained by securing equality of opportunity through legal reform to remove discriminatory provisions.
Welfare	Pertains to level of material welfare of women, relative to men, with respect to food supply, income and medical care, without reference to whether women are themselves the active creators and producers of their material needs.

Longwe also distinguishes between

Women's issues	Which pertain to equality with men in any social or economic role and involving any of the levels of equality
and	
Women's concerns	Which pertain to women's traditional and subordinate, sex-stereotyped gender roles.

The women's empowerment framework identifies three levels of recognition of women's issues in project design:

Negative level	Where project objectives are silent about women's issues. Experience suggests that women are likely to be left worse off by such a project.
Neutral level	Where the project objectives recognise women's issues but concern remains neutral or conservative, merely ensuring that women are not left worse off than before.
Positive level	Where project objectives are positively concerned with women's issues and with improving the position of women relative to men.

The framework can be used to produce profiles as below:

Levels of Recognition *Levels of Equality*	*Negative*	*Neutral*	*Positive*
Control			
Participation			
Conscientisation			
Access			
Welfare			

Women's Empowerment Framework for a Country Programme

Level of concern with women's development						
Sector	*Project*	*Welfare*	*Access*	*Conscientisation*	*Participation*	*Control*
Agriculture						
Education						
Industry						
Women's projects						

Uses of the Framework

- Particularly useful for groups committed to promoting equality and empowerment through their work.

Strengths of the Framework

- Develops the notion of practical and strategic gender needs into a progressive hierarchy.
- Shows that empowerment is an essential element of development and enables assessment of interventions along this criterion.
- Has a strong political perspective, aims to change attitudes?

Potential Limitations

- Assumption of levels of equality as strictly hierarchical is questionable.
- Framework is static and takes no account of how situations change over time.
- Examines gender relations from the point of view of equality alone, excludes interrelationship between rights, and responsibilities.
- Ignores other forms of inequality.

[Adapted from *Training Workshop for Trainers in Women, Gender and Development, June 9-21, 1996*, Programme Handbook, Royal Tropical Institute, The Netherlands.]

D. Social Relations Framework

The social relations framework originated with academics led by Naila Kabeer at the Institute of Development Studies at Sussex, UK. It is outlined in her book, *Reversed Realities: Gender Hierarchies in Development*, Verso, 1994.

Aims of the Framework

- To analyse existing gender inequalities in the distribution of resources, responsibilities, and power.

- To analyse relationships between people, their relationship to resources and activities, and how they are reworked through institutions.
- To emphasise human well-being as the final goal of development.

Features

The framework is based on the idea that the aim of development is human well-being, which consists of survival, security and autonomy. *Production* is seen as oriented not just to the market, but also to human well-being, including the reproduction of human labour, subsistence activities, and care for the environment.

Poverty is seen to arise out of unequal *social relations*, which result in unequal distribution of resources, claims and responsibilities. *Gender relations* are one such type of social relations. Social relations are not fixed or immutable. They can and do change through factors such as macro changes or human agency. Social relations include the resources people have. The poor, especially poor women, are often excluded from access and ownership of resources, and depend upon relationships of patronage or dependency for resources. Development can support the poor by building solidarity, reciprocity and autonomy in access to resources.

Institutions ensure the production, reinforcement and reproduction of social relations, and, thereby, social difference and inequality. Gender inequality is reproduced, not just in the household, but through a range of institutions, including the international community, the state and the market. *Institutions* are defined as distinct frameworks of rules for doing things and *organisations* as the specific structural forms that institutions take.

Gender analysis therefore entails looking at how institutions create and reproduce inequalities. There are four key institutional sites: the state, the market, the community and family/kinship.

Institutional location	*Organisational/structural form*
State	legal, military, administrative organisations
Market	firms, financial corporations, farming enterprises, multinationals
Community	village tribunals, voluntary associations, informal networks, patron-client relationships, NGOs
Family/kinship	household, extended families, lineage groupings

Five dimensions of institutional social relationships are especially relevant for gender analysis:

- *Rules*, or how things get done; do they enable or constrain? Rules may be written or unwritten, formal or informal.
- *Activities*, or who does what, who gets what, and who can claim what. Activities may be productive, regulative, or distributive.
- *Resources*, or what is used and what is produced, including human (labour, education), material (food, assets, capital), or intangible resources (goodwill, information, networks).
- *People*, or who is in, who is out and who does what. Institutions are selective in the way they include or exclude people, assign them resources and responsibilities, and position them in the hierarchy.
- *Power*, or who decides, and whose interests are served.

Institutional analysis reveals how gender and other forms of inequality are produced and reproduced.

Naila Kabeer classifies development policies as follows:

Gender-blind

- do not distinguish between men and women
- incorporate existing biases
- tend to exclude women

Gender-aware

- recognise differences among men and women's needs and priorities,

Gender aware policies may be of three types:

gender-neutral	• in light of gender differences, target delivery to men and women's practical gender needs • work within existing gender division of resources and responsibilities
gender-specific	• in light of gender differences, respond to the practical needs of men or women specifically • work within existing gender division of resources and responsibilities
gender redistributive	• intend to transform existing gender relations to create a more balanced relationship • may target both men and women, or one specifically • work on practical gender needs in a transformatory way • work on strategic gender needs

Finally, the social relations framework analyses *immediate*, *underlying* and *structural* causes of specific gender issues and their effects, as shown in the table below:

Analysis of causes and effects	
Long-term effects	
Intermediate effects	
Immediate effects	
The Core Problem	
Immediate causes at level of • household • community • market • state	
Intermediate causes at level of • household • community • market • state	
Structural causes at level of • household • community • market • state	

Uses of the Framework

- Can be used from project to policy level planning, even on an international basis.

Strengths of the Framework

- Sees poverty as not just material deprivation but also social marginalisation.
- Conceptualises gender as central to development thinking, not an add-on.
- Links micro to macro factors.
- Highlights interactions between various forms of inequality: gender, class, race.
- Centres analysis around institutions; highlights the political aspects of institutions.
- Dynamic; tries to uncover processes of impoverishment and empowerment.
- Can be used for different levels of analysis.

Potential limitations

- Since it examine all cross-cutting inequalities, gender can get subsumed under other analytical categories.
- Can appear complicated, detailed and demanding.

[Adapted from *Training Workshop for Trainers in Women, Gender and Development, June 9-21, 1996*, Programme Handbook, Royal Tropical Institute, The Netherlands.]

References

Advocacy Institute (2002): www.advocacy.org/pdf/9 Questions.pdf

Advocacy Institute (2004): http://www.advocacy.org/pdf/ issue_life_cycle.pdf

Bailey & Brake (1980): Radical Social Work and Practice, London: Edward Arnold

Bailey R & Brake M (1975): Radical Social Work, London: Edward & Arnold

Batten, T. R. and Batten M. (1967): *The Non-Directive Approach in Group and Community Work*, London: Oxford University Press, quoted in Mayo, M, Community Work in Hanvey C & Philpot T (eds), 1994, Practicing Social Work, London: Routledge

Beazley H & Ennew J.: (2006): Participatory Methods and Approaches: The Two Tyrannies in Desai and Potter (eds.) *Doing Development Research*

Beetham, D. (1992): *'Liberal Democracy and the Limits of Democratization'* in D. Held (ed.) *Prospects for Democracy. North, South, East, West*, Cambridge: Polity

Blankenberg F (1994): Monitoring and Evaluation of Networks, The Hague, NOVIB

Bon. L. (1910): The Crowd: A Study of the Popular Mind, London: George Allen and Unwin in Toseland RW & Rivas RF. 1995. *An Introduction to Group Work Practice*. Massachusetts: Allyn and Bacon.

Brett Lane & Diane Dorfman (1997): Strengthening Community Networks: The Basis for Sustainable Community Renewal, http://www.nwrel.org

Buchanan James B. & Tullock G. (1965): The Calculus of Consent. Ann Arbor: *University of Michigan Press* quoted in Singh, 1994, *Managing Common Pool Resources* OUP: Delhi

Calouste Gulbenkian Foundation (1968): *Community Work and Social Change. A Report on Training*, London: Longman.

Camilleri P. (1999): Social Work and its Search for Meaning, Theories, Narratives and Practices, in Fook and Pease: Transforming Social Work Practice, Post Modern Critical Perspectives, London: Routledge

Cartwright, D. (ed) (1968): Group Dynamics: Research and Theory, New York: Harper and Row

Celestine Nyamu-Musembi & Andrea Cornwall (2004): What is the "Rights-Based Approach" all about? IDS Working Paper 234

Chambers R. (1992): Rural Appraisal: Rapid, Relaxed and Participatory, IDS Discussion Paper 311

Chambers R. (1994a): Participatory Rural Appraisal (PRA): Analysis of Experience, World Development, Vol 22, No 9, Great Britain: Pergamon

Chambers R. (1994b): The Origins and Practice of Participatory Rural Appraisal, World Development, 22(7)

Chapman, J. (2002) Monitoring and Evaluating Advocacy. PLA Notes, 43: 48-52

Clarke, David B. (1973):The Concept of Community—A 'Re-Examination', The Sociological Review, 21 (3), August

Cohen & Uphoff (1980) : Participations Place in Rural Development, Seeking Clarity through Specificity, World Development, Vol 8

Cortes, E., Jr. (1993): In Henry G. Cisneros, (Ed.) Interwoven Destinies: Cities and the Nation. New York: W.W. Norton & Company

Council for Social Development (2006): 'India: Social Development Report, New Delhi: OUP

Cox E (2002): The Social Audit Cookbook, Lance Reichstein Foundation, University of Technology: Sydney

Craig, (2004) in Shaw M. (2004): Community Work, Policy, Politics and Practice, Hull: University of Hull and Edinburgh

Croft & Beresford (1989): User Involvement, Citizenship and Social Policy, Critical Social Policy, 26, 9(2) in Hanvey & Philpot (ed),1994, Practicing Social Work, London: Routledge

Croft & Beresford (1994): *A Participatory Approach to Social Work,* in Hanvey & Philpot (ed),1994, Practicing Social Work, London: Routledge

David N. Thomas (1983): The Making of Community Work, London: George Allen and Unwin.

Davis K (1961): Human Society, New York: MacMillan

Emma, G (2002): Neighbourhood Development in Guatemala City. Development And Change.31.5

Eyben (2004): 'Political and Social Inequality' Review Essay IDS Development Bibliography, 20, Brighton: Institute of Development Studies

Eyben (2003): The Rise of Rights : Rights Based Approaches to International Development, IDS Policy Briefing, 17, Brighton: IDS

FAO: Participatory Research for Sustainable Livelihoods: A Guide for Field Projects on Adaptive Strategies

Fook J & Pease B (1999): Post Modern Critical Theory and Emancipatory Social Work Practice in Fook & Pease: Transforming Social Work Practice, Post Modern Critical Perspectives, London: Routledge

Frankenberg (1957): Village on the Border, Cohen and West: London

Freire P. (1970): Pedagogy of the Oppressed, Harmondsworth: Penguin

Fukuyama (1995): Trust: The Social Virtues and the Creation of Prosperity. New York: Free Press.

Galpin, C.J (1915): The Social Anatomy of an Agricultural Community. Research Bulletin 34. Madison, WI: Agricultural Experiment Station: University of Wisconsin.

Gardner, J.W. (1995): National Renewal, National Conference on Governance

Gough I. (1979): The Political Economy of the Welfare State, London: The MacMillan Press.

Government of India (1987): Encyclopedia of Social Work in India, New Delhi: Publications Division

Gulbenkian Study Group Report (1968): Community Work and Social Change, London:Longman

Gulbenkian Study Group Report (1973): Community Issues in Community Work, London: Routledge and Kegan Paul

Hambly-Odame, H. (2000): Engendering the Logframe. ISNAR.

Hardin (1968): The Tragedy of the Commons, Science, 162: 1243-8

Harper, E. H. and Dunham, A. (1959) Community Organization in Action. Basic Literature and Critical Comments, New York: Association Press.

Healy K (2001): Reinventing Critical Social Work: Challenges from Practice, Context and Postmodernism, Critical Social Work, Vol. 2, No. 1, www.criticalsocialwork.com

Hillary, G. (1995): Definitions of Community: Areas of Agreement, Rural Sociology

Human Rights Council of Australia (2001): The Rights Way to Development—A Human Rights Approach to Development Assistance—Policy and Practice, Maroubra: The Human Rights Council of Australia

IDS (1996): IDS Policy Briefing Issue 7, http://www.ids.ac.uk

IDS (1998): Policy Briefing, Issue 12, November, http://www.ids.ac.uk

IFAD, ANGOC & IIRR (2001): Enhancing Ownership & Sustainability: A Resource Book on Participation: International Fund for Agricultural Development, Asian NGO Coalition for Agrarian Reform and Rural Development & International Institute for Rural Reconstruction.

International Institute for Environment and Development (1996): Participation, Policy and Institutionalisation. PLA Notes No. 27. London: IIED

Jain L.C. (1985): Grass Without Roots, Rural Development Under Government Auspices, New Delhi: Sage

Junior A.P., Atunes M. and Romano J. (2004): Linking Rights and Participation: Brazil Country Study, Action Aid Brasil, www.ids.ac.uk/ids/particip/rights

Karl M. (ed)(1999): Measuring the Immeasurable, Planning, Monitoring and Evaluation of Networks, New Delhi: Women's Feature Service

Krishna & Shrader (2000): 'Cross Cultural Measures of Social Capital: A Tool and Results from India and Panama' Social Capital Initiative Working Paper Series No 21, Washington DC :The World Bank

Ledgerwood J. (1998): Sustainable Banking with the Poor, Washington DC: World Bank

Ledwith Margaret (1997): Community Development, A Critical Approach, Bristol: Policy Press

Leonard, P. (1975): Towards a Paradigm for Radical Practice, in Bailey R. & Brake M. (eds) Radical Social Work, London: Edward & Arnold

Lewin K. (1947) Frontiers in Group Dynamics. *Human Relations*. 1. 2-38.

Lindeman, E. (1921): The Community: An Introduction to the Study of Community Leadership and Organization, New York: Association Press

Ljungman Cecilia M. (2005): A Rights-Based Approach to Development in Britha Mikkelsen, Methods for Development Work and Research—A New Guide for Practitioners, Sage Publications: New Delhi

MacIver R.M. & Page C.H. (1961): Society, MacMillan: London

Mayo, M. (1994): Community Work, in Hanvey C & Philpot T. (eds), Practicing Social Work, London: Routledge

Mckean, M.A. (1987): Success on the Commons: A Comparative Examination of Institutions for Common Property Management; A Paper Presented at a Conference on Advances in Comparative Institutional Analysis at the Inter-University Centre of Post Graduate Studies at Durham, quoted in Singh Katar 1994 , *Managing Common Pool Resources*. OUP: Delhi

Midgley et al. (1986): Community Participation, Social Development and the State, London: Methuen

Midgley, J. (1995): *Social Development. The Developmental Perspective in Social Welfare,* London: Sage.

Mikkelsen B. (1995): Methods for Development Work and Research, A Guide for Practitioners, New Delhi: Sage

Morales A. & Sheafor B.W. (1989): Social Work, A Profession of Many Faces, Toronto: Allyn & Bacon

Moreau M. (1979): A Structural Approach to Social Work Practice, Canadian Journal of Social Work Education, 5 (1)

Mukherjee N. (2002): Participatory Learning and Action, New Delhi: Concept

Mulgan Geoff (1997): 'A Sense of Community', Resurgence, No 172, quoted in Rahnema, Majid: Towards Post Development: Searching for Signposts, A New Language and New Paradigms, in Rahnema M. & Bawtree V., The Post Development Reader, London: Zed Books

Mullaly R.P. (1993): Structural Social Work: Ideology, Theory and Practice, Ontario: McClelland & Stewart

NABARD (Undated): Participatory Self Monitoring System for Self Help Groups

Narayan D. (1999) Bonds & Bridges: Social Capital and Poverty. Washington DC: The World Bank. Mimeo

NASW (1973): Standards for Social Service Manpower, Washington DC: NASW

O'Connor J. (1973): The Fiscal Crisis of the State, St James Press, quoted in Gough I, 1979, The Political Economy of the Welfare State, MacMillan: London

Oakley, P. et al. (1991): Projects with People: The Practice of Participation in Rural Development. Geneva: International Labour Organisation

Olson (1965): The Logic of Collective Action: Public Goods and the Theory of Groups, Harvard University Press, quoted in Singh K & Gain RTS. 1995. *Evolution And Survival Of Self Help Groups: Some Theoretical Propositions And Empirical Evidences*, Paper Presented at the International Seminar on Development of Rural Poor through Self Help Groups, NABARD

Parsons T. (1951): The Social System. New York: The Free Press

Pateman, C. (1970): Participation and Democratic Theory, Cambridge: Cambridge University Press

Paul (1987): Community Participation in Development Projects, World Bank Discussion Paper 6, Washington DC: World Bank

Paul Shaffer (1995): Poverty Approaches, in Poverty Research Unit Newsletter, AFRAS, Univ of Sussex, Autumn.

Pettit & Musyoki (2004): Rights, Advocacy and Participation—What's Working? Participatory Learning and Action, 50, Sussex, IDS

Putnam (1993)(b): The Prosperous Community: Social Capital and Public Life. The American Prospect, 13, 35-42.

Putnam (1995): Bowling Alone, America's Declining Social Capital. Journal of Democracy, 6:1 Quoted in G Emma. 2002. Neighbourhood Development in Guatemala City. Development and Change, 31.5

Putnam, R. (1993)(a): Making Democracy Work: Civic Traditions in Modern Italy. Princeton: Princeton University Press

Putnam, R. D. (2000): Bowling Alone. The Collapse and Revival of American Community, New York: Simon and Schuster.

Rahnema, M. (1992): 'Participation', in W. Sachs ed. 2000:The Development Dictionary: A Guide to Knowledge as Power, New Delhi: Orient Longman

Richmond M (1917): Social Diagnosis, New York: Russel Sage Foundation

Ross, Murray G. (1955): Community Organisation: Theory, Principles and Practice, New York: Harper & Row

Rothman, J. (1968) 'Three Models of Community Organization Practice' in Social Work Practice, New York: Columbia University Press.

Samaranayake M. (2001) in IFAD, ANGOC & IIRR: Enhancing Ownership & Sustainability: A Resource Book on Participation, International Fund for Agricultural Development, Asian NGO Coalition for Agrarian Reform and Rural Development & International Institute for Rural Reconstruction, 2001

Samuel J. & Jagadananda (2003): Social Watch India, Citizens Report on Governance and Development, CYSD & NCAS

Samuel J. (2002): What is People-Centred Advocacy? PLA Notes, 43: 9-12

Schech S. and Haggis I. (2000): Culture and Development, A Critical Introduction, Oxford: Blackwell

Shepard, C (1964): Small Groups: Some Sociological Perspectives, San Francisco: Chandler Publishing.

The World Bank, 'What is Social Capital? PovertyNet http://www.worldbank.org/poverty/scapital/whatsc.htm

Thomas David N. (1983): The Making of Community Work, London: George Allen & Unwin.

Toseland R.W. & Rivas R.F. (1995): An Introduction to Group Work Practice. Massachusetts: Allyn and Bacon

Twelvetrees (1991): Community Work (2nd ed), London: MacMillan

UNDP (2000): Human Development Report, New Delhi: Oxford University Press

UNDP (2002): Handbook on Monitoring and Evaluation for Results, UNDP: New York

UNDP Empowering People: A Guide to Participation, http://www.fao.org/Participation/english_web_new/content_en/project_part.html

United Nations (1971): "Popular Participation in Development: Emerging Trends in Community Development", New York: U.N.

United Nations (1981): Popular Participation as a Strategy for Planning Community Level Action and National Development, New York: United Nations.

United Nations (1986): Declaration on Right to Development, www.unhchr.ch/html/menu3/b/74.htm

White (1974): Community Work in a Local Authority, London, Association of Community Workers

Wilensky & Lebeaux (1965): Industrial Society and Social Welfare, New York: Free Press

World Bank (1996) World Bank Participation Sourcebook. Environmental Management Series, Washington DC: World Bank

Younghusband, E. L. (1959): Report of the Working Party on Social Workers in the Local Authority Health and Welfare Services, London: HMSO

Websites

www.advocacy.org
www.cashpor.com
www.criticalsocialwork.com
www.fao.org
www.ids.ac.uk
www.infed.org
www.nwrel.org
www.unhchr.ch
www.worldbank.org

Index

Absolute poverty, 178
Accountability, 34-37, 40, 68, 79
Advocacy, 77-78, 95
  issues, 81
  messages, 80
AIDS orpans, 8
American Association of Social Workers, 1
Andrea, C., 36
Anti-poverty, 203
Assessing Women's needs, 197

Bailey, R., 9
Baseline data, 139
Batten, T.R., 28
Battle against poverty and hunger, 42
Beazley, H., 126
Below poverty line, 6
Beneficiaries, 65
Birth control, 41
Blankenberg, F., 146
Bon, L., 58
Borrowing pattern, 194
Bourdieu, Pierre, 17
Brett Lane, 16
Buchanan, James B., 60
Budget allocation, 88
Bureaucracy, 5

Calouste Gulbenkian Foundation, 23
Camilleri, P., 8
Cartwright, D., 59
CASHPOR House Index (CHI), 185-87
Catholic Community, 12
Celestine, N.M., 35
Challenges, 2, 11, 70
Chambers, Robert, 61, 62, 63
Chapman, J., 83
Child beggars, 8
Child mortality Rates, 22
Chinese Community, 12
Christian Community, 12
Clarke, David B., 12
Cohen, 45, 46
Cohesion, 59
Coleman, James, 17
Colonial Community development work, 25
Colonialism, 172
Communications, 79
Communication skills, 127
Commonity action, 27
Community affiliation, 15-16
Community development, instruments of, 17
  programmes, 6, 43, 54
Community forestry project, 57
Community infrastructure, 176-77
Community negotiating strategies, 16
Community organizations, 17-18, 22-23, 25-28
Community Resource map, 99
Community structue, 175
Community work, definitions of, 24
  methods of, 28
  models of, 26
  states of, 95
Community and Community Work, 11-12

Conceptualization, 3, 35, 45
Conscientisation model, 44
Conservatism, proponants of, 11
Constraints, 71
Consultation, 52
Convention on the Elimination of All Forms of Discriminal against Women (CEDAW), 29
Convention on the Rights of the Child (CRC), 29
Coronations, 13
Cortes, E., 18
Cost-of-basic needs Method (CBN), 178
Crisis, 8
Critical consciousness, 44
Critical issues, 29
Critical social work, 10
Criticism, 41
Croft, 39

Daily activity clock, 111-12
David, H., 153
Davis, Kingsley, 14
Decentralisation, 54
Declaraton on the Right to development, 170-72
Demographic challenges, 8
Differences between conventional and participatory evaluation, 150
Direct observation, 129-30
Discrimination, 69
  against girl child, 7
Disparities, 5
Dramatic occurrences, 13

Economic Commission of Latin America (ECLA), 45
Economic development, 41
Economic policy, 7
Economic problems, 5
Economic rationalism, 11
Elective communities, 12
Employment, 190
Empowering participation, 47
Empowerment, 31, 204
  evaluation, 161-63
Engendering participatory monitoring and evaluation, 154-55
Ensuring transparency, 71
Environmental issues, 37
Ethno-methodological approach, 126
Evaluation planning, 161
Export growth, acceleration in, 7
Export-led economic growth, 5
External crisis, 8

Facilitating questions, 102, 105, 120
Facilitators, 141
Family life crisis, 13
Farming occupation, 102
Feminist social work models, 9
Flexibility, 75, 136
Focus group meetings, 133-34
Food aid distribution, 68
Food/crops, subsidies for, 5
Food energy method (FEM), 178
Food production, 41
Food security and Nutrition status, 140, 192
Food share method, 178
Fook, J., 9
Foreign exchange, 7
Functional participation, 47, 49, 50
Fundamental communal elements, 13

Galpin, C.J., 12
Gardner, J.W., 16
Gender Focussed issues, 192-93
Gender sensitive monitoring, 155
General Assembly Resolution, 168
Globalization, 7, 8
Gough, I., 4
Group learning, 76
Guinean society, 180
Gulbenkian Foundation Reports, 26
GTZ, 38

Hambly-Odame, H., 156
Hardin, 61

Harvard Analytical framework, 196
Health status, 190-91
Healy, K., 10, 11
Help Local Communities, 72
Hindu patriarchal ideology, 7
HIV prevention, 161
Household composition, 189
Household expenditue, 194
Household interviews, 133
Human development, process of, 30
Human Rights approach, 30-31
Human Rights Council of Australia, 35
Human Rights Organisation, 32
Human Rights treaty, 33
Humanitarian, 29

Ideal community, 15
Immunization programme, 153
Indifferent between participate and stakeholders, 115
Individual tragedies, 13
Industrialization, 15
Information, 139
  participation by, 51
Information technology revolution, 7
Institutional formulation, 3
Institutional policies, 25
Institutional social relations, dimensions of, 210
Institutionalisation, 29
Interactive participation, 51
International Bill of Rights, 29
International Covenant on Civil and Political Rights (ICCPR), 29
International development agencies, 32, 55
International Federation of Social Workers, 29
International financial community, 5
International Monitory Funds (IMF), 5
International Peace and Security, 170, 173
Involving people challenges institutionalised discrimination, 40
IFAD, 38

Jagadananda, 6
Jain, L.C., 43
Joint planning, 52
Jules, N., 49

Karl, M., 85, 86, 145
Key informant interviews, 131-32
Key principles, 74
Krishnamachari, V.T., 43

Leadership development, 25
Learning attitudes, 71, 136
Ledgerwood, J., 153
Ledwith, M., 45
Legitimacy, 79
Leonard, P., 9
Lewin, Kurt, 58
Liberalisation, 7-8
Life cycle state, issues of, 83-83
Lindeman, E., 15, 22
Linking PRA to Community Work, 93-94
Literacy, 139, 189-90
Local communities, 71, 145
Local development activities, planning and implementation of, 87
Local institutions, 175
Locality development, 25
Logframe, 156
Logical Framework Approach (LFA), 88-90

MacIver, R.M., 13, 14
Macro-economic reforms, 5
Magical consciousness, 44
Maharashtra Rural credit programme, 147
Managerialism, 11, 36
Manifestations, 31

Manipulative participation, 48-49
McKean, Margaret A., 60, 61
Mental discipline, 134
Mexico, 5
Mickkelsen, B., 52, 54
Micro-credit programme, 138
Migration, 102, 140, 194
Minimum needs programme, 6
Mobility map, 113-15
Modern community, 14
Modern welfare state, 4
Modernisation, 27
  theories of, 41
Moderation, 134
Monitoring levels, 136-37
Monitoring and Evaluation (M&E), 135
  systems, 145, 151
Monotheism, 58
Morales, A., 2, 29
Moreau, Maurice, 9
Moser's Gender planning framework, 203
Mukherjee, N., 63, 64
Mulford conferences, 1
Mulgan, G., 22
Mullaly, R.P., 8, 9
Multinational Corporations, 7
Multiple perspectives/triangulations, 74
Muslim community, 12
Myrdal, Gunnar, 41

NABARD, 147
Narayan, D., 16, 180
Narayanan, K.R. (former President of India), 6
National Association of Social Workers (NASW), 2, 29
National health service, 4
Natural resources, 36
Negotiation, 69, 136
Networking, 85
New social movement, 8
Non-Governmental Organisations (NGOs), 40, 48, 85
Non-retrogression states, 33

Oakley, P., 47
Objectively verifiable Indicators, 93
Obligations, 31, 35
  types of, 37
Observation, aims of, 129
O'Connor, J., 5
Offsetting biases, 63, 72
Olson, 60
Optimising trade-offs, 63
Outcome mapping, 157-60
  development programmes, 158, 160
  methodology of, 157-60
Overall Community development, 105
OHCHR, 34

Pair-wise Ranking, 119-121
Panchayati Raj Acts, 87
Panchayati Raj Institutions (PRIs), 43, 54
Parent/Child relationship, 18
Parsons, T., 59-60
Passive participation, 50
Participation, 25-26, 40-48, 54-56
  conceptualization of, 45
  principle of, 34-35, 39-40
  stage typology, 49
Participation and Community Work, 36-37
Participatory approaches, 67, 126, 140
  overview of, 76
Participatory assessments, 152
Participatory attitudes, 70
Participatory baseline, 152
  advantages of, 142-43
Participatory Community Work, 96
  auxiliary and supplemental skills in, 77-78
Participatory development, 32, 46-47

Participatory decision-making, 71
Participatory evaluation, 151-55
activities of, 152
programmes, 149
responsibilities of, 181
Participatory Learning Action (PLA), 62
Participatory Mapping, 98-99
variants of, 99
Participatory Methods, 65, 91
Participatory Monitoring, 93, 137, 143-44, 152
benefits of, 144
problems of, 144
Participatory Monitoring and Evaluation (PM&E), 135
Participatory Poverty Assessment (PPA), 180
Participatory processes, 74
Participatory projects, 57
issues of, 144
Participatory Project Management, 88-89
Participatory Research, 125-28
methods of, 126-27
Participatory Rural Appraisals (PRA), 61-62, 182
techniques, 182
tools of, 96, 139
Participatory Self-Monitoring, parameters for, 147-49
Participatory strategies, logical models of, 53-54
Participatory tools, 139
Participatory Wealth Ranking (PWR), 182
Paternalism, 29
Pease, B., 9
People confered advocacy, 78
People centered development, 42
People's paticipation, inbuild component of, 36
Perennial occurrences, 13
Perlman's problem solving model, 2
Pettit, 65, 67
Political philosophy, 3
Poor and very poor, characteristics of, 179
Povety, 7, 30, 138, 178, 209
alleviation programme, 158
assessment, 181
causes of, 65
changes of, 32
pattern of, 69
Povety line, income/consumption method, 180
Privatization, 8
Poblem analysis chart, 123-24
Problem Tree Chart, 121-22
Professional Community Work, 24
Project cycle management, 56-59, 138
Project formulation, 105
Project identification and preparation, 155
Project planning matrix, 91
Public assessment, 88
Public expenditure, 5
Putnam, R., 16, 17

Quality of education, inequalities in, 7
Quasi-stationery eqilibrium, 58
Questioning route, 134

Racial discrimination, 172
Rapid Participatory Rural Appraisal (RPRA), 62
Rapid Rural Appraisal (RRA), 61-62, 182
Relationship between communities and institutions, 16
Relationship between disarmament and development, 170
Relationship between social work and welfare state, 8
Resource map, 99-100
formulation of, 105
Responsibilities, 79-80, 141
Reversals of Modes, 73

Richmond, Mary, 1
Rights-based approaches, 32-35, 70
Rights-based development strategy, 35
Roger's person-centered model, 2
Ross, Murray G., 22
Rural poor, rights to education, 6

Samuel, J., 6, 78
Saving pattern, 194
Scheduled Castes and Scheduled Tribes, 6, 37
Seasonal livelihood calendar, 108-110
Secondary data, 128-29
Self-critical awareness, 76
Self-determination, 28, 169, 172
Self-mobilization, 49
Semi-Structured Interviews (SSI), 130-31
Sexual exploitation, 68
Sexual orientation, 12
Sheafor, B.W., 29
Shepard, C., 58
Social audit, 86-87
  advantages of, 87
Social capital, 5-6, 16-20
  basic attributes, 19
  characteristics of, 20-21
  development of, 19-20
Social consumption, 5
Social development, issues of, 42
  strategy of, 41-42
Social exchange, 58
Social exclusion, 65, 69
Social expenses, 5
Social expenditure, 8
Social investment, 5
Social justice issues, 42
Social map, 100-104
Social mobilization, 55
Social network, 15
Social planning, 25-26
Social policy and planning in national development, 41
Social programmes, 41
Social relationships, 13
Social relations framework, 208-09
Social sector allocation, 7
Social security system, 4
Social transformation, 10
Social work, crisis in, 8
Social work goals, 40
Stabilization policies, 5
Stakeholders, 63, 150, 154, 181
State expenditure, categories of, 5
Stratification, 102
Structural adjustment programmes, 5, 7
Structural observation, 130
Structural social capital, 17
Structural social work, 10
73rd and 74th Amendment to Constitution of India, 37, 43

Technical methods, 25
Thomas, David, 23, 24, 27
Toreland, R.W., 61
Trafficking, victims of, 8
Transformation, 97
  programmes, 38
Transect walk, 104-05
Transitive participation, 48
Transparency, 79
Trend line, 117-19
Triangulation, 107
Twelvetrees, 25

Underdevelopment, examination of, 45
  problems of, 41
Unemployment, 8
Universal declaration of Human Rights, 29, 30, 36, 66, 164-67
Universal primary education, 57
Uphoff, 45, 46
Urban Local Bodies, 54
Uttar Pradesh, 22

Venn diagram, 91, 96, 115-16, 117
Violence, 32
Violations, 172
Visual sharing, 75

Visualisation in Participatory Programme (VIPP), 62
Voluntary agreement between free individuals, 4

Watershed development, 36
Welfare programmes, social control functions of, 9
Well-being analysis, 106-07
White, 12
Wilensky, 3
Women's activities, project impact on, 198
Women's empowerment framework, 205-08
World Bank, 5, 21, 38

XY-axis graph, 118

Younghusband Report, 23